PRATTVILLE
❧ A L A B A M A ❧

PRATTVILLE
ALABAMA
A BRIEF HISTORY *of* THE FOUNTAIN CITY

MARC PARKER &
MELISSA BENEFIELD PARKER
FOREWORD BY JIM BYARD JR.

Charleston · London

THE
History
PRESS

Published by The History Press
Charleston, SC 29403
www.historypress.net

Cover design by Natasha Walsh

First published 2012

Manufactured in the United States

ISBN 978.1.60949.194.9

Library of Congress CIP data applied for.

*Melissa dedicates this book to her parents,
James and Azell Benefield.*

*Marc dedicates this book to his dad, Harry Parker,
and grandmother Tura Floyd.*

CONTENTS

FOREWORD

This typical hot and humid summer day in June 1999 found me, a thirty-two-year-old young man, standing in the Daniel Pratt Cemetery, overlooking historic downtown Prattville, about to embark on a course that would forever alter my life. You see, in just a few hours, I was to be sworn in by the governor as mayor of the city of Prattville, Alabama.

The Daniel Pratt Cemetery is a wonderful spot of God's earth and is a place that allows for peaceful reflection in the quiet shadows of the gravesites of Pratt and his close family members. The cemetery literally sits atop a hill and gracefully looks down on the city that Pratt built. So, as I stood there thinking of the awesome task and responsibility that I would shoulder, my mind turned to Daniel Pratt, the man who many years earlier had mapped out the plan for my hometown.

This great industrialist was on many folks' minds back in 1999, as that was the year that marked his 200th birthday; furthermore, the state had proclaimed 1999 as the "Alabama Year of Industry," to coincide with Prattville's year-long Daniel Pratt Celebration. Prattville is known as the "birthplace of industry" in Alabama, largely due to the industry that Pratt founded around 1839.

Later that very day, after I was sworn in, I remembered the words of Daniel Pratt: "Whatsoever thy hand findeth to do, do it with all thy might." I was completely unaware that I would be serving almost twelve years as the city's chief elected official. Little did I know that we would experience triumphs as well as tragedies—both good and bad times. But what I did know as the mayor and leader is that I would, in the words of our founder, "do it with all [my] might."

Being mayor of your hometown is a wonderful job. It's a job that I loved. It's a job that if you're going to do well, you have to love. Even during the most challenging of days, I enjoyed my service to the citizens of Prattville. The city saw tremendous growth in population and business during my time as mayor. Population growth saw a considerable increase between 2000 and 2010 of about ten thousand people. In 1999, Prattville had many national fast-food chains and retailers, but by 2010, we were home to most national restaurants and had become a retail shopping destination of Alabama's River Region that featured the state's first Bass Pro Shops store erected in 2007.

By 2010, the city had revitalized the Daniel Pratt Historic District's business district with several drainage and streetscaping projects. We created a creek walk feature along the Autauga Creek and as a community have always carried a strong emphasis on character and quality of life.

Folks often ask, "What was the toughest part of being mayor?" Of course, it is difficult to answer that question, but the absolute darkest days of my time as mayor began on August 16, 2001. That was the day that an eleven-year-old girl, Shannon Paulk, went missing. Several months later, it was discovered that Shannon had been abducted and murdered. This innocent child's death changed our city forever.

We had three damaging and costly flood events during my years as mayor, and on September 10, 2002, downtown Prattville's landscape was altered forever by a fire that totally gutted the massive three-story, two-block-long historic Gurney Manufacturing facility.

Mother Nature visited the city with devastating intensity on February 17, 2008, when an EF3 tornado ripped across several eastern Prattville residential neighborhoods and business districts. Thankfully, no lives were lost. The late Scottish minister and teacher Oswald Chambers once said, "We imagine we would be all right if a big crisis arose; but the crisis will only reveal the stuff we are made of, it will not put anything into us. Crisis always reveals character." Our city's true character was revealed that Sunday afternoon in February and in the days that immediately followed when the citizenry of Prattville responded with outstretched hands and open hearts to the victims of this catastrophe.

In addition, our administration would have been unsuccessful without the aid of the city employees working tirelessly alongside me. I was also blessed to serve with able city councilmen who should be given much credit for the growth of Prattville.

Mayor Jim Byard. *Courtesy of Marc Parker.*

My job allowed me to meet and interact with people from all walks of life, from the average citizen with an issue to the secretary of defense visiting nearby Maxwell Air Force Base. I always enjoyed getting to know the people I was privileged to serve, and city council meetings were a means to that end. It was at one such meeting that I first met Marc and Melissa Parker. Little did I know that we would become friends or that they would publish and operate an online news publication and subsequently be asked to author a nationally published book on the history of Prattville. As I transitioned to Governor Robert Bentley's cabinet in January 2011, it was photographer Marc Parker who chronicled my final hours as the chief officer of the city.

I would enjoy talking with Daniel Pratt. I would enjoy walking with this indomitable, indefatigable man around the downtown historic district that bears his name. It would be a pleasure to drive him around the new growth areas of the city and show him the progress that has been made. It would be fascinating to hear Pratt's thoughts and revelations about his town.

When he plotted Prattville similar to his New England hometown of Temple, New Hampshire, Pratt planned areas of industry, residences, churches, schools and parks. In doing so, his concern for the citizens showed not only in their work lives but in their civic lives as well. I am hopeful that Pratt would be pleased with the concern shown to the citizens today. For we, in Prattville, continue to work, live, play, worship and exist in the shadows cast so long ago by Daniel Pratt. Our founder and first mayor or intendant (as they were called during Pratt's era) lived by the mantra: "No criterion, but success." It is my desire that Pratt would have judged that over two hundred years later, the mantra during my time at city hall remained the same.

Jim Byard Jr.
Prattville Mayor (1999–2011)
Director of Alabama Department of Economic and Community Affairs
(2011–present) for Governor Robert Bentley

ACKNOWLEDGEMENTS

We wish to state that the historical information contained herein has been verified with several sources. Many interviews were conducted for the purposes of adding flavor and color to the book. Some Prattville residents are fortunate enough to be able to weave a tapestry of tales about the ancestors who walked the roads before them. Quotes from these interviews are the personal comments and opinions of these gracious people and are not necessarily the views shared by us, nor are they necessarily historically accurate. Legends, folklore and/or rumors of any kind are just that and meant to be taken with a grain of salt for entertainment purposes; naturally, they cannot be construed as the absolute truth in every single case.

Our sincere thanks is offered to each and every person who assisted in the creation of this book, particularly the following people: Prattville mayor Bill Gillespie and mayor's executive assistant/webmaster Teresa M. Lee; former mayor Jim Byard Jr., who wrote the foreword and spent much time with us reminiscing about his early days in Prattville over coffee at Jim's Restaurant; former Continental Eagle Corporation vice-president Dave Mrozinski, who whiled away many hours of his valuable time in long conversations about cotton gin manufacturing; historian and former Continental Eagle Corporation employee Tommy Brown, who shared his encyclopedic knowledge of the city; Autauga County circuit clerk Whit Moncrief and his wife, Jamie, two good friends who shared many memories of Prattville's past; the former director, Robin Hughes, and the current director, Rachel Deaile, of the Autauga County Heritage Association, who both so graciously left us alone to search and dig; with special gratitude to Rex Musgrove and former police chief Alfred Wadsworth, without whom the book would be missing priceless old photographs.

Many people were called upon to assist, and we appreciate each and every one who complied. If we have omitted anyone from the following thank-you list, please accept our sincere apologies and know that it was definitely not intended.

In no particular order, thank you to former mayor Gray Price and his wife, Julie; councilman Willie Wood Jr.; former council president Mike Renegar; former council president Dean Argo and councilman Nathan Fank; city planner Joel Duke; former fire chief Stanley Gann; former Alabama state legislator H. Mac Gipson; International Paper Company employees Susan Poole and Martin Peters; former Prattville Chamber of Commerce president Jeremy Arthur; executive director of the Prattville Autauga Character Coalition Mary Anne "Boo" Rogers; Jimmy and Dot Sanford, Katherine Porter; Nelda Cain; Verda Cain; Susan Cranfield; Delois Sager; Jennie Burt; Rosie Houser; Emma Warren; Guy Boutin; Sam and Mary Lou Abney; and last but certainly not least, the grand storyteller Gene Kerlin.

Please keep in mind that this is a "brief history" of Prattville, with the emphasis on brief. While we wanted to include absolutely everything about the city's past, present and future in this book, our limited word count set by the publishers made that virtually impossible, so certain aspects or events of Prattville's history had to be omitted from the manuscript.

INTRODUCTION

Prattville was called the Fountain City because of its many artesian wells that produced drinkable water. A 1933 edition of the *Prattville Progress* noted that there were more than four hundred of these wells in the city and its immediate vicinity, some of which supplied the town's water system. Several of them ceased to flow when efforts were made to move the wells in later years, but many still produce gallons of sweet, free-flowing water daily. Citizens and visitors can sip from a well in the backyard of the Prattaugan Museum, at Heritage Park overlooking Autauga Creek and the historic gin complex or under a tin-roofed shed on Doster Road and enjoy the delicious artesian water.

Former Prattville mayor Jim Byard Jr. said of his hometown:

Cities are living breathing things, so you're either moving forward, or you're stagnating or you're moving backwards. I've heard people say, "I wish Prattville would stay the same." My mom always said she wanted Prattville to stay like it was when I was little, but she says that she wants a Parisian and a Lowe's. Well, you can't have those without moving forward. I want Prattville to remain what I think its hallmark is across the state right now. When people think of Prattville, they think of a very progressive community, a clean place, the hometown of the River Region, and that's what I want us to remain as. As we grow population-wise, we have to make sure that we nurture the quality of life like horticulture or cultural arts. Those are easy things for someone to cut out of a budget, but those

Gin complex. *Courtesy of Marc Parker.*

are the lifeblood of the city. That's what makes us unique because we have those amenities that are offered to our citizens, and you don't notice them until they're gone.

Prattville, Alabama, is the quintessential American city, tucked in the foothills of the Appalachians. This town of nearly thirty-five thousand is mere minutes from the capital city of Montgomery. "The Fountain City" is not unlike the fictional town of Mayberry depicted on *The Andy Griffith Show*. Life is simple here. Faith and family are the primary focus of the citizens in this quaint New England–styled southern village. Sunday mornings are filled with worship, and Friday nights in the fall are spent cheering on the beloved nationally prominent Prattville High School Lions football team.

Bill Gillespie Jr., the current mayor of the city, epitomizes this ideal. He is a lifelong Prattville resident, born and raised in the city, and grew up in the family tire business, which remains in operation today. He has spent several years as a youth league umpire, and it was this public service that spawned future political aspirations because he wanted to be in a position to improve life for the hometown youngsters. By his own admission, this mayor is not a career politician, just an everyday guy trying to make a small difference in the lives of his citizens. In doing so, Gillespie is continuing the overarching theme of Prattville's founder, New Hampshire native Daniel Pratt, who, about 175 years ago, made the city a place where families could worship, prosper and recreate.

1

PRATTVILLE FOUNDER DANIEL PRATT

Builder and Architect

Prattville founder Daniel Pratt, the man who was called "Alabama's first great industrialist" for his contribution to the burgeoning cotton gin industry, was born in the tiny town of Temple, New Hampshire, on July 20, 1799, to Edward and Asenath (Flint) Pratt. He was the fourth in a family of six children, with sisters Asenath, Dorcas, Abigail and Eliza and only brother Edward.

Pratt's parents managed to support the family on the meager income from a small farm, but the children attended school only in between planting and garnering seasons. It was impossible financially for the young Pratt to attend college, but he had a remarkable mind and strong will nonetheless. He decided, at sixteen years old, to learn a trade under the apprenticeship of skilled carpenter Aaron Kimball Putnam, who lived in the neighboring town of Wilton. When Putnam fell into financial trouble, Pratt asked to be released from his apprenticeship to seek work in the South, which was then known as the land of opportunity. If successful, he vowed to return and pay Putnam's debts. Pratt was let go from his apprenticeship, and he sailed to Savannah, Georgia, in 1819 to begin his southern career as a builder.

Upon arriving in Savannah with only twenty-five dollars and his tool chest, Pratt put all the skills he had learned from Putnam into building homes in the seaport mecca; however, he did not immediately become a rich

Daniel Pratt. *Courtesy of Library of Congress.*

entrepreneur, even though he designed and built homes for wealthy planters and moved on to shipbuilding to expand his knowledge of construction and the industrial process. Nevertheless, the young man earned enough to redeem the mortgage on Putnam's home as he had promised. After a couple years' experience in design, and with considerably more money in his pocket than when he reached Savannah, Pratt headed to Milledgeville, a place that was becoming increasingly prosperous, mostly due to the fact that it was the antebellum capital of the state.

Pratt gained much fame and notoriety from designing homes in the city of Milledgeville, which was about 165 miles inland from Savannah. Local master builder John Marlor hired him in 1821, and together they were responsible for many of the Federal-style homes that line the city's streets, referred to locally as "Milledgeville Federal."

Over the next ten years, Pratt plied his trade in the vicinity of Milledgeville and nearby cities and dominated the building and contracting business in the area. He was also successful on a personal level when he met Columbia, Connecticut native Esther Ticknor, who was on vacation visiting relatives in Jones County. The two wed on September 6, 1827, and a few years later headed for Clinton, a booming town in the heart of a cotton-growing area in Georgia. The city was also the trading center for as many as sixteen thousand people and had four springs of freely flowing water that not only supplied people, horses and travelers but were also used for manufacturing purposes—and Pratt had the idea of manufacturing cotton gins.

Cotton Gin Manufacturing

An early Clinton, Georgia pioneer was Samuel Griswold from Burlington, Connecticut. Like Pratt, he was a skilled carpenter and mechanic. Griswold made a small start in the tinware trade, selling articles he produced, before progressing to the much more lucrative business of producing cotton gins. Griswold hired Pratt to operate his newly established gin manufactory and soon made him a partner in the business. The gins sold quickly in a short period of time, but Pratt urged his partner to expand the business into Alabama because the Georgia cotton belt seemed limited and static.

Apparently not wanting to take a chance on moving the lucrative business and fearing trouble from Alabama's Creek Indians, Griswold declined his partner's invitation to move the factory to a location on the Alabama River, a site that would have given him much greater access to the booming southwestern market. Pratt and his wife packed up their belongings, along with enough material to build fifty gins, and headed west to wild, practically uncharted Alabama, which was just thirteen years into statehood.

In 1833, after a long and tedious journey, the group arrived at Elmore's Mill about sixty miles from Wetumpka, Alabama. Pratt assembled his material and realized that it was still easy to sell his cotton gins, but he would not be satisfied until he found an abundant water source to provide power for a factory. The next location he chose was known as McNeil's Mill on Autauga Creek. Pratt easily produced about two hundred gins a year at this location and marketed them throughout southern Alabama, but demand for cotton gins was great. The indomitable spirit that kept pushing him to succeed throughout his life now drove him to seek more land to house a larger gin factory.

In late 1835, Pratt purchased approximately one thousand acres of land on Autauga Creek, four miles from Washington, at about twenty-one dollars an acre from Joseph May, to be paid in four installments between 1836 and 1838. The property included a small sawmill. He now had his large space, available water power and the abundance of yellow heart pine in the surrounding hills for the construction of the gins, so he set out to build his manufacturing facilities and plotted a town along the banks of the Autauga Creek. Pratt's goal was to build a town that resembled a northern manufacturing village, one similar to those in his home state of New Hampshire.

Despite the dilapidated and dismal land conditions and the naysayers who couldn't believe he had purchased such a mess, Pratt immediately began the arduous process of draining the marshes near the creek to transfer his operations to the new site. Shadrack Mims, Pratt's close friend and factory worker, remarked that the land was valuable for nothing except its pine timber and said that the location was little else than a quagmire that cost thousands of dollars to drain to be fit for any kind of building: "Mr. Pratt did an immense amount of work on the place. It was very sickly while the ditching was being done."

A few years before Pratt's arrival, Autauga County's population totaled more than 50 percent slave, and the slaves provided the necessary physical labor to aid Pratt in clearing the land—in essence, to create the town of Prattville. After the area was rid of trees and other obstructions, Pratt established a sawmill, a gristmill and later a flourmill. The early growth of the city was indeed centered on the Pratt Gin Factory; thus, the profits from this economic cornerstone financed the beginnings of other industries, such as the sash, door and blind factory, a wagon manufactory and a blacksmith shop. (It would be worth mentioning at this juncture that a cotton gin is a machine that quickly and easily separates cotton fibers from seeds.)

Former Continental Eagle Employee and historian Tommy Brown noted, "Wherever the cotton gins were, that was the social area of the town, where everyone gathered."

According to the journal the *American Cotton Planter*:

> *Of Mr. Pratt's gins, we can say to our readers in want of a first-rate stand, unhesitatingly—and we say so without prejudicing any other factory—*

Gin complex. *Courtesy of Rex Musgrove.*

that, with all his late improvements and the advantages afforded by his large factory arrangements, he is able to furnish the neatest, most complete and best cotton gin stand in America.

Some gins were standard, and some were made to order. Often, the planters of the Mississippi River Valley ordered gins of special construction with extras. Many were elegant and resembled the loveliest pieces of parlor furniture rather than simply having the appearance of an ordinary machine for a plantation. Pratt sold to Russia, the British Empire, France, Cuba, Mexico and Central and South America, as well as across the South. All of the materials used in the construction of the gins, except the sheet steel for saws, were southern. The sheet steel was imported from Naylor's Steel Works in Sheffield, England, because it was a better grade of steel than that found in the United States.

In addition to manufacturing, the factory also repaired gins, and it usually had more than it could handle during cotton-harvesting season, which was August through December each year, with August being the busiest month as planters were preparing for harvest. Pratt and other machinists sometimes spent a couple of days traveling to places repairing gins. Replacement parts for gins were also sent out from the factory. Work was abundant. Pratt could now afford to build a home that was spacious enough for a growing family.

The Pratt Home

The Prattville founder chose a location on the western bank of Autauga Creek, about two hundred feet northwest of his gin factory. The house was not as lavish or ornate as the dwellings he built in Georgia for wealthy landowners, but this one was spacious and featured a sunken brick wine cellar, brick stables, a large wing to house the servants' quarters and, in later years, an orchard, vineyard and art gallery that housed work by his favorite painter, George Cooke, who specialized in portrait and landscape paintings.

Cooke, a Maryland native, toured Europe for several years, actually focusing on Italy, learning and copying the paintings of the Renaissance master artists. These copies were then sent to the United States because Americans might otherwise not have a chance to see these great works of art. Two paintings that adorned Pratt's walls were *Interior of St. Peter's, Rome* and *The Last Supper*.

Pratt basically opened up his art gallery so that the citizens of the town could view and appreciate the canvassed scenes of passed grandeur and greatness. Many hours could be spent there enjoying the work of Cooke and other artists. Portraits of George Washington, Henry Clay and Bishop Soule were also displayed.

Tommy Brown noted:

> *The large deep pink crepe myrtle to the right front of the Continental Eagle Corporate Office is a tree from the old Pratt home. The hillside opposite the Continental Eagle parking lot on Gin Shop Hill Road is still terraced where the ten acres of Daniel Pratt's grapes were grown.*

Daniel Pratt home. *Courtesy of Rex Musgrove.*

Regrettably, the Pratt family home was torn down in the 1960s, and that was the impetus for establishing the Autauga County Heritage Association a few years later. It is a dire shame that the people of Prattville lost this cherished heirloom of the town's history.

Gene Kerlin, a Prattaugan museum volunteer, recalled:

> *At the time, the headquarters* [Continental Gin] *was in Birmingham. They decided they would relocate the headquarters to Prattville, and they needed a place to build the office building, so they cleared off land, and the Pratt house was razed. It was torn down about 1962.*

Expanding the Family and the Factory

Three children were born to Pratt and Esther, but only daughter Ellen survived infancy. Ellen, born in 1844, would later elope in 1863 with her father's ward and business protégé, Henry DeBardeleben. At the time of Ellen's death a month after reaching her fiftieth birthday, she was survived by eight children. Esther was forty years old when she gave birth to Ellen's sister Mary in 1843, and that child died the same year. Maria was born in 1847 and passed away two years later. While the Pratts were grieving these personal losses, the family gin business continued to grow and show large profits.

In 1851, Prattville had approximately eight hundred inhabitants, with almost every family having a member employed in one of Pratt's enterprises. The demand for cotton gins increased from other states, and in 1854, out of necessity, Pratt constructed a new brick factory, three stories high, which had a capacity of making 1,500 gins annually. The first floor held the machinery, breasting and finishing department, testing of gins operated from the second floor and the third floor housed painting and varnishing. An elevator, likely fueled by water power, took gin parts and partial and complete gins floor to floor.

In a letter to a friend on July 19, 1954, Daniel Pratt wrote:

> *I find my old gin shop too small. It is getting a good deal worse for wear. I find I should have to stop to repair or build now, therefore, I've concluded to build a new shop which I am now doing, expect to be able to move into it next year. I am building it on the west side of the creek. I am putting it up of brick, two hundred and twenty feet long, fifty feet wide with a wing thirty-four by forty all three stories high. I am expecting to put in the best of machinery and to have the best cotton gin factory in the world. Several years since I put up a brick building where the old gristmill was about two hundred and thirty two feet long, twenty-nine feet wide, three stories high. I use this for sash door and blind business, a machine shop for the foundry and a carpenters shop. I am getting old (fifty-five tomorrow), must quit building. I think, however, that our village will continue to improve slowly. We have five stores here, all I believe doing well. Have a printing office, three churches and two schools.*

Surprisingly enough, Pratt secured no patents on his gins until June 1857. Then his patent consisted, as he described it, of a gin so constructed that "a spiral movement is given the cotton within the box or hopper and a fresh surface constantly presented to the saws, so that the cotton will be stripped from the seed without being cut or broken." He secured other patents after the Civil War, but his genius as a gin manufacturer lies not in the patents he secured but in the large-scale production of a popular and superior gin, which he constantly improved during the period when such a gin was necessary if the cotton kingdom were to expand from South Carolina and Georgia to Texas.

By 1860, Pratt employed sixty-six workers at his gin company, which was a much larger workforce than in other pre–Civil War manufacturing towns, and the Prattville plant was producing 1,500 gin stands per year. In that year, there were fifty-seven gin manufacturers in the United States, and only three were in the South.

The company diversified product lines throughout the nineteenth century and expanded production to include cotton condensers, feeders, elevators and presses. It began producing the Munger gins as well as the Pratt gins. Robert S. Munger made a fortune and a sizable reputation for himself by improving Eli Whitney's cotton gin. All of these changes and additions necessitated another plant expansion, so in 1898, some twenty-five years after Pratt's death, the masonry building was erected to house heavy metal fabrication and for assembly of feeders and condensers.

This was the largest gin factory in the world, and Pratt's gins were renowned wherever cotton was grown. The factory was also still in use for producing cotton gins until recently, when the owner, Continental Eagle

Gin complex. *Courtesy of Marc Parker.*

Corporation, ceased operations in January 2012. The buildings are some of the earliest brick industrial structures in Alabama.

Tommy Brown noted, "People do not understand that *this* is not a cotton gin. The factory *builds* cotton gins and always has built cotton gins. You can say a factory is a mill, but Daniel Pratt called it a manufactory."

A genuine cotton gin that was built at the Daniel Pratt Gin Company was donated in 2010 to the Autauga County Heritage Association by Will Crenshaw, a Butler County Farmers Federation member. It was used by his great-grandfather Frederick William Crenshaw III on the family farm many years ago and can be seen at the Prattaugan museum in Prattville today. The story goes that his great-grandfather bought the gin directly from the Pratt Gin Company in the late 1890s on a trip to Prattville and shipped it back on the train to Greenville in Butler County, Alabama. It was hauled to the gin house by wagon. The gin clearly bears a July 15, 1873 patent, and "DP" is stamped on the grease trap doors. Old gin records appear to indicate November 1898 as its date of manufacture. Autauga County Heritage Association board member Ann Boutwell's long search for an old Pratt gin ended when she checked the markings and completed some research. The verdict was: "It's a Pratt!"

Prattville Manufacturing Company

The cotton mill boom that occurred briefly in the South during the 1820s, and with great force during the 1840s, was, in part, the southern response to too much dependence on the North for manufactured goods and financial and commercial services. That's why Pratt built his city with industries at the center, modeled after villages in New England. He believed that if the South stayed a purely agricultural economy, it would never progress or create wealth and would forever remain dependent on the North.

Autauga was one of several counties known as cotton plantation counties, and it paid two-thirds of the state taxes collected from the then fifty-one counties. In antebellum Alabama, wealthy planters created large cotton plantations based in the fertile black belt—a region underlain by a thin layer of rich, black topsoil—and depended on the labor of enslaved African Americans for the operation. The manufacture of cotton was of great interest in this region in the 1830s and '40s. In 1842, the *Huntsville Herald* reported that several bagging and rope factories were being built in Jackson County and that there were four cotton factories in operation in Madison County (north Alabama) alone.

The development of the cotton textile industry was not without its setbacks, however; in 1840, the Bell Factory of Patton Donegan Company in Madison County was burned with a loss of $40,000, with only $20,000 insurance. Described as one of the most extensive factories in the South, the Globe Factory of Martin and Cassity, also in north Alabama near Florence, was destroyed by fire, with an uninsured loss of $15,000.

By the late 1840s, many planters had become desperate over the continuing downward spiral of cotton prices. One planter wrote to the *Alabama Planter* (published in Mobile, Alabama), saying, "Cotton raising is a rather uncertain and unprofitable calling. It is a little like gold digging, yet I do not know what else to engage in unless I build a factory." His hope, of course, was that someone with the capital would partner with him to use his water power site because it was believed that such a factory would pay for itself in a year and a half.

In 1846, Pratt further expanded *his* industrial complex by founding and organizing the Prattville Manufacturing Company (PMC), and the buildings were erected several years later. He built this textile mill on the east side of Autauga Creek, adjacent to his cotton gin factory.

The labor for the mill came from the poor white families of the county who were given homes at very low rental cost. The average wage paid to the two hundred men, women and children of the factory was eight dollars a month. Another New Hampshire native, Jesse Perham, served as the first mill superintendent but proved quite unsuccessful and left Prattville not long after PMC began operating. Pratt found a new, well-qualified superintendent on a trip to Rhode Island. Gardner Hale was a man with good moral judgment and integrity who was instrumental in developing what is now known as Bluff Park in Hoover, Alabama. The mill performance improved vastly under Hale's guidance, and he would stay at PMC until after the Civil War.

By 1850, this textile factory of Pratt's employed 136 operatives who worked 2,800 spindles and 100 looms to produce $85,000 worth of coarse cloth annually. Later in the decade, Pratt added 485 wool spindles to produce additional coarse cloth for slave clothing, which kept his factory operating during hard times. Under Pratt's leadership, the Prattville Manufacturing Company became one of the most successful and well known of the cotton and woolen mills in the antebellum South, and a national business journal recognized Prattville as the most highly

Gin complex, early 1900s. *Courtesy of Rex Musgrove.*

Wool mill covered bridge. *Courtesy of Rex Musgrove.*

Red Arrow Hardware. *Courtesy of Marc Parker.*

industrialized village of its size in the United States. Alabama had twelve cotton mills during this time, employing 715 people and processing 5,208 bales of cotton each year. Ten years later, the number of mills was only fourteen, but the amount of cotton being raised had doubled and the number of workers had increased.

The mill supplied Confederate uniforms to the Prattville Dragoons, the first company of men from the city of Prattville and Autauga County to form for service in the Civil War. They were made of black broadcloth trimmed with gold braid and were said to be the best-looking uniforms in the state. Pratt also donated about $17,000 for horses and saddles and purchased hundreds of thousands of Confederate bonds to help the cause of promoting states' rights.

Tommy Brown recalled:

> *A man whose family rented Daniel Pratt's house said that he played in the attic when he was a child and that there were boxes of black uniforms there. The Prattville Dragoons' uniforms were black wool. He remembered them being military uniforms.*

The historic Red Arrow Hardware building located in downtown Prattville was once used by Pratt as a cotton warehouse for the Prattville Manufacturing Company. The front entrance led into a cotton storage area surrounded by an open shed.

Philanthropist

Pratt was Alabama's first millionaire.
—former Continental Eagle Employee and Historian Tommy Brown

Pratt accumulated a huge fortune from his gin factory and other industries before 1860, and he became Alabama's first person to earn $1 million in an industrial enterprise. He was manufacturing no fewer than 1,500 cotton gins per year and making over $500,000 a year from various enterprises, and he lived in a mansion built on a thirty-acre plot on a lofty hill with a picturesque view of his beloved Autauga Creek.

Living a comfortable lifestyle in his namesake town, Pratt also became a well-known philanthropist, donating large sums to the Methodist Church and to state and private institutions of higher learning in Alabama and Georgia. He gave $500 to a Prattville man whose home had burned and was known for many benevolent acts of kindness to strangers and friends. Pratt was even responsible for opening the first school in the city, the Male and Female Academy, in order to offer a sound education to the children of his millworkers, and after the Civil War, he continued to provide employment and charity to the needy and the freed blacks during the Reconstruction period.

Shadrack Mims noted:

> *Mr. Pratt was not an avaricious man, grasping money to hoard up. He knew no other use for money than to make it subserve a valuable purpose, to give employment to the laboring poor. This, I think, was his purpose from first to last and his great success in business is, no doubt, due to the purity of his motives in keeping everything and everybody astir. That he possessed a good judgment, indomitable perseverance and good management, no one can doubt. He was firm and decided and had nerve to risk capital when judgment dictated.*

Pratt contributed largely to the building of the first Autauga County Courthouse, completed in 1870, and provided lots for the Baptist and Presbyterian churches and the town cemetery. According to R.G. Dun, the first successful commercial reporting agency in America, Pratt had, by 1853, already given as much as $100,000 for charitable purposes. After the Civil War, when the art gallery building attached to his home had to be razed due to dry rot, Pratt donated the two largest paintings, *Interior of St. Peter's, Rome* and *The Last Supper*, to the University of Georgia. *Interior of St. Peter's, Rome* was placed in the university chapel, where it can be seen today.

Daniel Pratt was not only the largest gin manufacturer in 1860, but he also operated a successful textile mill, foundry, flour mill, wagon manufactory, tin shop and sash, door and blind factory. His gross income of more than half a million dollars during this period was living proof that industry could be even more lucrative in the South than the cultivation of cotton and that this man transplanted from a tiny New Hampshire village definitely had the Midas touch. But even more than that, Pratt loved his town, the state of Alabama and the South.

In an 1849 newspaper article entitled "Present Position of Alabama," Daniel Pratt wrote:

> *I contend that any business which brings capital to the State improves it, and that which is for the interest of the State is for the interest of its citizens. As an instance, I will merely cite the little village which I founded some nine years since. When I made purchase of the place, I presume it did not pay a tax exceeding fifteen dollars, and had there been no manufacturing done there, the tax would now probably exceed twenty dollars. This year it paid from five to six hundred dollars tax, half of which goes to our county. Suppose some ten villages should spring up in the county, the tax derived from them would pay all our county expenses and leave the tax collected from our citizens to be invested in a school fund. The founding of manufacturing villages throughout the state would serve materially to lessen our taxes and give besides employment to a large number of persons who are dependent on their daily labor for a support of their families. To effect all of this, we want a few good stock banks, well managed, and my word for it, such improvements would go on gradually until our State would command as high a position as any in the South.*

Birmingham and Pratt City

Alabama's antebellum economy was predominantly agricultural and limited industrial development by the time of the Civil War. In the early 1870s, Pratt purchased thousands of acres of land in north Alabama, and he and his son-in-law, Henry DeBardeleben, acquired controlling interest in the Red Mountain Iron and Coal Company. The duo also purchased the Oxmoor furnaces that had been destroyed in the war and chose to develop the Helena, Alabama mines in order to rebuild the state's industrial economy. Daniel Pratt reflected, "I well know I cannot expect to live to see the mines in operation, yet I want to start that business as the last act of my life for the good of my adopted state."

Pratt had great confidence in his son-in-law's ability to carry this project and placed DeBardeleben in charge of the difficult reconstruction at a time when economic disasters plagued Birmingham. DeBardeleben had only worked iron up into gins and had never set eyes on the raw product, but at about thirty years old, he was energetic and impulsive and set about this new adventure with zest.

Pratt biographer S.F.H. (Susan Frances Hale) Tarrant wrote:

> It was undertaken reluctantly on account of his age and infirmity, for he (Pratt) doubted if he should live to witness its completion, yet his State pride urged him to undertake it. He believed something should be done to develop the mineral resources of the state. He thought labor should be diversified in order that the South might sustain herself. For this enterprise, he felt great solicitude and remarked a few days before his last illness, "If it is the will of God, I should like to see the completion of this enterprise."

Early in the spring of 1873, the Oxmoor furnace went into blast, and Pratt was ill and close to dying, but he rejoiced over the fact that the reconstruction work, by which he hoped the South would gain new life, partly by means of his own earnings and by the work done by his son-in-law, would reach completion. He lived just long enough to see his experiment turn out its first pig iron in Jefferson County, Alabama.

After Pratt's death, DeBardeleben continued in the iron and coal business under the name of Pratt Coal and Coke Company. Realizing the importance of the "Pratt Seam" of coal, DeBardeleben named it after his late father-in-law. Alabama's earliest and largest mining boomtown was Pratt City, located just north of downtown Birmingham. Pratt put up the money to start the town, and Scottish mining engineer and executive Erskine Ramsay, along with hundreds of miners, extracted the black gold. By 1890, the town boasted four thousand people drawn from all across the South, the northern industrial centers and foreign nations to find work, and as mining, coke and shipping operations expanded, Pratt City also developed as a regional center for the outlying coal mining towns.

The deadliest tornado outbreak to hit the United States in forty years occurred on April 27, 2011, and at least one tornado spread a wide path of destruction in Pratt City, leaving the community virtually in ruins. Houses were reduced to rubble while cars were thrown around like feathers before being slammed to the ground by the twisters. The scene was eerily similar to the destruction of war. It has been a long recovery process, but a year later (2012), homes have been rebuilt, a new fire station was erected and a new senior citizen home is planned, as is a new library.

The End of an Era

In 1866, Pratt was elected by 98 percent of the voters (176 of 177) to serve as intendant of Prattville, a position that holds the same responsibilities as that of mayor, and he also served in the Alabama House of Representatives from 1861 to 1865. He continued to work constantly and drive himself in the late 1860s and 1870s, even as his health steadily worsened. In 1872, he complained to his good friend, finance agent and bookkeeper Shadrack Mims, that he had "been laid up about two weeks not able to attend to business. My hand is so lame now, I am hardly able to hold a pen."

That absorption with his work and impetus to succeed, however, gives an incomplete portrait of the man. Pratt never forgot the devout teachings of his parents and balanced his devotion to business with a commitment to family, friends and the community at large. His strong ties to his relatives can be traced through the rest of his life from his 1827 letter to his father: "You may depend, I respect you as a father and believe that I think of you as often as you do of me."

Alabama's industrial pioneer, builder of one of the most extraordinary towns in the antebellum South and Prattville's first mayor passed away

Postcard depicting the gin complex. *Courtesy of Rex Musgrove.*

on May 13, 1873, just two months shy of his seventy-fifth birthday. As the *Prattville Signal* newspaper reported on May 15, 1873:

> *For the first time during the existence of our paper, now stretching back into the past through more than twenty years, we clothe our columns in the sable habiliments of mourning. Daniel Pratt, the founder and builder of our town, is no longer numbered among the living. He died after a long, lingering and painful illness soon after the break of day on Tuesday morning last.*

"Blessed are the Dead who lie in the Lord, for they rest from their labors, and their works do follow them," are the words inscribed on the north face of Pratt's monument, and on the west side of the monument facing Esther's grave is inscribed, "Even so Father, for it seemeth good in thy Sight." Daniel Pratt chose for his family cemetery the site on a hill overlooking his residence and his village.

The entire town mourned the death of not only the founder but also the constant and faithful friend of Prattville and all its interests. The busy hum of industry was hushed, and all houses of businesses were closed. The bells no longer summoned industrious toilers from labor to refreshment

Downtown, early 1900s. *Courtesy of Alfred Wadsworth.*

but only tolled in solemn requiem over the honored dead. Every heart was oppressed with the sadness of a common grief that fell over the entire community. The town and its inhabitants were so near and dear to Pratt's heart. There was not one individual there whom he had not directly or indirectly benefited. They mourned together the loss of a fellow citizen, a neighbor and a friend.

Daniel Pratt's cotton gin factory became the largest in the world even before the start of the Civil War. His name became synonymous with cotton operations, and the man established Prattville as one of the antebellum South's most celebrated manufacturing towns. Pratt's invincible pioneer spirit is just as highly esteemed today in the twenty-first century as it was when this brave God-fearing man traveled by horse-pulled wagon from the east to the very young, wild state of Alabama.

On February 22, 1999, Alabama senator Richard C. Shelby declared:

> *I rise today to pay tribute to Daniel Pratt, a distinguished Southern Industrialist and founder of the city of Prattville, Alabama; a man whose vision guided the state on a course of industrialization and*

modernization. As a celebration of Daniel Pratt's 200th birthday, 1999 has been named the "Year of Industry" in Alabama. Daniel Pratt's legacy not only includes the beginning of modern industry to the state, but also philanthropic deeds that were unrivaled for his era. As his first biographer, Shadrack Mims wrote: "The indomitable will of Daniel Pratt, that spirit of enterprise which characterized him through life, was not to be daunted nor discouraged by Indian uprisings. He purchased material for fifty gins, put the same on wagons, and in 1833, he with his brave wife headed to Alabama."

Daniel Pratt's birthday is celebrated annually on July 20 in the town that he built. The mayor places a wreath on the grave of Prattville's founder, whose gin factory became the largest producer of cotton gins in the world. Pratt is buried in his family cemetery, just off Gin Shop Hill.

Daniel Pratt Left His Mark on Prattville and the South

Daniel Pratt is considered the South's first industrialist. He began the large-scale manufacturing of cotton gins after Eli Whitney's patent expired. In the late 1830s, he laid out the foundation of Prattville and built his cotton factory and gin factory. By 1860, the latter had reached the capacity for making 1,500 gins. Pratt added a flour mill, a wool factory, an iron foundry, a sash and blind factory and a lumber mill. During his lifetime, Prattville's founder pioneered many industrial operations that are still flourishing today.

In the general development of the cotton textile industry of Alabama, there were three outstanding Alabama promoters: Henry Watkins Collier, chief justice and governor of Alabama, the earliest to make a strong plea for the extension of the textile industry; Daniel Pratt, probably the most noted manufacturer in the state, who urged planters to buy at home and stop sending their money to the North; and James Martin, owner of the largest cotton manufacturing mills of the antebellum period, who called on all southerners to contribute their abilities to the development and growth of diversified industry.

Downtown, looking west. *Courtesy of Rex Musgrove.*

In 1847, the University of Alabama conferred on Pratt the degree of master of mechanical and useful arts as "a token of respect and honor felt by the trustees, in common with reflecting men in every station, for that high degree of intelligence, benevolence, uprightness and success which you have exercised and displayed," as the letter from President Manly expressed it. Pratt was saluted for supporting schools for the working man as well as the rich and also for supporting religious institutions.

Even though Pratt was not able to bring a railroad to Prattville, he was proud of his town, which was known for having good morals and good society. The Prattville Ladies' Aid Society was formed in May 1866 to raise funds for the relief of destitute Autauga County war widows and orphans, and it worked hard to raise money through charity suppers, bazaars and concerts and actually making clothes for needy children by hand.

Pratt was the candidate for his party for state senate from Montgomery and Autauga in 1855 and was defeated, but from 1861 to 1865, he represented the county in the lower House of the legislature. He was as well known for his piety, integrity and hospitality as for his energy and enterprise.

In addition to the cotton mill in Prattville, Pratt acquired landholdings in north Alabama that became famous coal and ore mining industries and built furnaces near Birmingham to make iron from the red ore deposits in the mountains around the area. The furnaces were destroyed by Wilson's Raiders in the war, but Pratt and his son-in-law, Henry DeBardeleben, rebuilt them. Although a severe financial panic hit the United States in October 1873, Pratt died earlier that year, but lived to see iron being made at the Oxmoor furnaces from the red ore and coal from Alabama mines.

2

NOTABLE FIGURES
WHO PAVED THE WAY FOR
PRATTVILLE'S BEGINNING

Daniel Pratt's Wife, Esther Ticknor

Daniel Pratt married Esther Ticknor in 1827 after only a short courtship, but the union lasted almost forty-six years. Esther's prominent New England family included William Davis Ticknor, a partner in a Boston publishing company whose firm handled an impressive list of authors, including Horatio Alger, Charles Dickens, Ralph Waldo Emerson, Harriet Beecher Stowe and Mark Twain. One of Esther's cousins was Francis Orray Ticknor, a physician and poet born in Jones County, Georgia. He was best known for his Civil War piece, *Little Giffen of Tennessee*, the purported true story of Isaac Newton Griffin, who was cared for by the Ticknors after being wounded in the bloody conflict.

From historical accounts, the Connecticut native decided to stay in Prattville when her husband offered to take her back to familiar surroundings and their relations in the North; therefore, Esther actually should be given a substantial amount of credit for the establishment of the town. Not only did her decision to remain in the South play a valuable role in the creation of Prattville, but available evidence also suggests that the couple had an uncommonly strong marriage and that Daniel placed great faith on Esther's judgment, with her cheerful, serene nature possibly calming some of his more tempestuous moods, especially exemplified during business hours.

Esther was actually an ideal helpmate to her husband, and Pratt's new brothers-in-law, Samuel, Simon and John, followed the future industrialist to Alabama to invest their time, money and talents into his gin business, while Esther involved herself in many benevolence projects in Prattville. While her husband would walk around the village visiting families and urging the importance of punctual attendance at church, she would supply suitable clothing for mill children so that they would not be too embarrassed to attend Sunday school classes. Esther died on February 14, 1875, about two years after her beloved spouse; her estate was divided between her son-in-law and daughter, Henry and Ellen DeBardeleben, and nephew Merrill Pratt.

Samuel Griswold, Pratt's Partner in Georgia

At twenty-two, Samuel Griswold married Louisa Forbes in Burlington, Connecticut. Three children—Roger, Lucia and Elisha Case—were born to the couple. The family moved to Clinton, Georgia in 1818, and shortly thereafter, Griswold began work as a store clerk to save capital for a business he was planning to build because his family quickly expanded with the addition of Giles, Mary, Annie, Elizabeth and Ellen.

About 1828, after opening a factory in Clinton manufacturing cotton gins, Griswold built the first frame dwelling in the town near the courthouse and for several years used it for a store and a dwelling. A couple of years later, Griswold met up with another early Clinton settler, Daniel Pratt, and hired him as a factory superintendent. Pratt's carpentry skills no doubt helped perfect the wooden framing and cabinets of the Griswold gin stands; thus, the two entrepreneurs were partners within a year in the thriving business.

When Griswold declined Pratt's invitation to head west to possibly make the business even more successful, the Georgia cotton gin pioneer purchased about five thousand acres of land along the Central of Georgia Railroad (often called the Georgia Central), at a point about two miles south of his original base at Clinton and ten miles east of Macon, and founded a township suitably called Griswoldville. Now having the advantage of rail transport, Griswold was able to build an enormous factory that produced cotton gins; a sawmill; a gristmill; and factories that made bricks, soap, furniture and candles. He also erected a large family home, houses for his children and in-laws, a church, a post office and about sixty cottages for his slaves and workers.

By 1849, Griswold was selling eight hundred gins per season and was expanding into the northwestern section of the state. He and his son Elisha entered into a new business with Pratt called Samuel Griswold and Company, but this lasted only three or four years. In the late 1850s, Griswold began experiencing failing health due to circulatory problems.

Griswold suffered a debilitating stroke during this time and basically deferred all business affairs to his son Giles, who supervised the family's farming operations, but the gin manufacturing became outmoded during the Civil War. Agricultural machinery was less needed than weaponry, and the Griswolds had to change with the times. Similar to Daniel Pratt, who aided the war effort by making Prattville Dragoon uniforms in his factory and donating money for arms and horses, Griswold allowed his town to be used as a camp and training ground and furnished the local hospital with beds and coffins. From April to June 1862, his factory shipped about eight hundred pikes to the state armory in Milledgeville. After that delivery, however, Griswold turned his attention to a much more valuable addition to the Confederate arsenal: a replica of the Colt 1851 revolver named Griswold & Gunnison.

Arvin W. Gunnison was an employee at Griswold's cotton gin factory but left to become a gun manufacturer in New Orleans. He returned to Griswoldville after the fall of New Orleans in the war. Gunnison and Griswold became co-owners in the pistol works firm and developed a replica of the .36-caliber Colt Navy revolver, which was a favorite of cavalrymen.

At first glance, their weapon could actually be mistaken for a Colt original, but a main difference was that the Colt used steel on the frame and trigger guard instead of brass mixed with copper content, which was used on the G&G pistol because of a shortage of graded steel in the South. Griswold and Gunnison revolvers were sold to the Confederate army for the exorbitant price of $40.00 each, while Samuel Colt was selling his top-quality 1851 Navy revolvers for a reasonable $13.75 each.

The gun production came to an end during the Battle of Griswoldville, or what some call the "Gettysburg of Georgia," when men of a Georgia militia made a futile attack on Major General William Tecumseh Sherman's army. This was the first skirmish in Sherman's "March to the Sea." The town was destroyed in 1864 by the Ninth Michigan Volunteer Cavalry Regiment, and the gun factory was burned to the ground. Griswold died just three years later.

Early Prattville Settler and Biographer Shadrack Mims

Shadrack Mims not only worked for Pratt in several capacities at the gin factory, cotton mill and Prattville Mercantile (Pratt company store), but he and Prattville's founder were also confidants. Mims wrote about Pratt and the town's early days in *History of Autauga County, Alabama*. Not only do some historians credit Georgia native Shadrack Mims with the naming of the city of Prattville (others say it was another early settler named Amos Smith), but he was also cited as being Daniel Pratt's first biographer and wrote at length about the great industrialist's character.

Mims noted Pratt as being sometimes formal and distant, modest at all times and not caring for foolish jesting. The writer claimed that his boss and friend could have flashes of temper, be impatient and was a workaholic. On the other hand, Mims recorded several instances of Pratt's charity toward friends and strangers, generally aiding those in need and utilizing Christian principles in business to help his employees build strong moral fortitude. Mims wrote:

> *Having acted as Agent for the Prattville Manufactories for fifteen years, no one has a better knowledge of the amount of good done to the operatives and their families, both in a pecuniary way and in the improvement of mind, manners and morals. They are, at this time, a much higher grade of society than when they first came to the place. I am truly glad to know that the trustees of our school are advancing the educational advantages so that this class of people may now have a still better chance for intellectual improvement. The citizens of Prattville cannot do better for themselves than carry out the plans of Mr. Pratt as to their educational and religious interests—these two interests, if properly attended to, will assure respectability in this life and a blissful immortality in the next.*

Mims stated that Pratt's objective was to give employment to as many operatives as his means would justify and to furnish them with educational and religious advantages. He described the first schoolhouse that Pratt built as being located on the side of the hill southwest from the foundry and said that the seats were built on the Lancastrain plan—i.e., one above the other with desks complete, leaving a space in front for the teacher and recitations. The school was situated in a cool, sequestered place completely surrounded by a forest growth of young oaks and a cool spring running from the hill. An accomplished scholar and gentleman, T.B. Avery, taught the school on the Induction plan, which involved drawing out the mind and teaching it to be self-reliant.

Also included in *A History of Autauga County, Alabama* are personal incidents involving Mims and Pratt. One such story was a near-death experience for the two men. It happened as workers were engaged in digging out a cellar for a machine shop. They approached too near the brick foundation, and it gave way. Pratt and Mims were standing about fifteen feet away from the building on the creek bluff discussing building a brick dam where the old dam (built in 1839) stood. Suddenly, the building began cracking and crashing. Pratt escaped through the falling timbers, and Mims dove into the creek. Everyone escaped harm, and Mims found out later that Pratt could not swim; therefore, he chose not to escape danger by diving into the creek.

In addition to Pratt, Mims spoke of other early Autauga County pioneers and cited Amos Smith, a foreman at Pratt's gin shop, and Martin Ross Burt, who became a successful planter. The Burt home, built of heart pine, is still standing in Prattville today and is listed on the Alabama Register of Historic Places. Burt and his wife, Delilah, had fifteen children, nine girls and six boys. The stairway to the upper floor, where the girls slept, was in Martin's bedroom so he could count them as they retired. Mims wrote:

> *After crossing Autauga Creek, the first farm you came to belonged to Charles Booth, then Thomas Smith, then Thomas Coleman who had a mill on a creek two miles west of Prattville. Further on was the farm of Martin R. Burt who married Miss Griffice. She was a Methodist, and the whole family joined. Martin Burt was an industrious, thrifty, moneymaking man of good character. His children all did well. The Amos Smith family was remarkable for their steady, quiet and orderly lives. Honest, industrious, punctual and economical, they were all successful in business.*

Shadrack Mims married Elizabeth Dowsing probably about the time he arrived in Alabama. He spent his later years after retirement on his plantation and passed away on October 21, 1885.

According to "Death & Marriage Notices from Autauga County, Alabama Newspapers" by Larry E. Caver Jr.:

> *Mr. S. Mims died at his residence near Prattville on Wednesday evening last after a painful and lingering disease incidental to old age. He was about eighty-one years old and had spent the greater part of his manhood in this county, and no man was ever more universally beloved and respected*

Chapel at Old Prattvillage. *Courtesy of Marc Parker.*

by his fellow man for his upright conduct and Christian character than he. A noble, pure and upright man has fallen and taken his place with the redeemed who have gone before, leaving an example worthy of imitation by the young. Peace be to his ashes.

Elizabeth Mims died about eleven years later. The couple's son, Wilber, and his descendants operated a hotel on Third Street in Prattville until 1944. According to lore, the hotel was built by Pratt to be used as a boardinghouse for county locals staying in town overnight to conduct business or who showed an interest in Pratt's factories. It was the home of southern poet Sidney Lanier when he was the headmaster of the Prattville Male and Female Academy.

The Mims Hotel was moved to the present site in the city in 1982 and restored as part of Old Prattvillage commercial complex, which consists of a cluster of historic buildings and a small Gothic-style chapel that are located in the first block of First Street downtown. The little village began with efforts to preserve older structures in danger of being demolished, and the Autauga County Heritage Association worked to relocate the historic Mims Hotel to the area.

Charles Atwood, a Slave Belonging to Daniel Pratt

Most of the towns in the South had a cotton gin. Where the roads met, you would find a gin. The increase of the southern slave trade was a direct effect of the increase in cotton production brought by the invention of the cotton gin. The invention of the cotton gin is not the reason for slavery as many scholars suggest. There has never been an invention made by mankind that ever enslaved anyone. People enslave people, not machines.
—former Continental Eagle Employee and historian Tommy Brown

During the first half of the nineteenth century, cotton and slave labor were central to Alabama's economy. As of statehood in 1819, slaves accounted for more than 30 percent of Alabama's approximately 128,000 inhabitants. Daniel Pratt's father quickly admonished his son for purchasing slaves in an 1827 letter, to which the budding young industrialist gave him a sort of "When in Rome, do as the Romans do" philosophy and replied:

My slaves which you mention are not numerous. I did not intend that you should know anything about that as I supposed that you would think I was ruined eternally. I assure you that to live in any country, it is necessary to conform to the customs of the country in part. I have bought no man into bondage, and I am in hope I have rendered no man's situation more disagreeable than it was before, but on the contrary, I am in hopes that I have bettered it.

Historical accounts indicate that Daniel Pratt bought a slave named Charles from Samuel Griswold in 1843. Charles's mother was an African American, and his father was Caucasian. Later, Pratt bought a female slave named Eliza for Charles to marry. At the time, Eliza belonged to a family named Atwood, so Pratt adopted the name "Atwood" for Charles and Eliza. The newly named Atwoods were more accepted as servants to Pratt instead of slaves because Charles served as a coachman and personal valet to the founding family.

Nellie Atwood Strong, Charles Atwood's granddaughter, recalled:

Charles was a mulatto, the son of a white man. The Pratts were not used to owning slaves. My grandfather had it softer. They must have been pretty nice to him. Eliza belonged to the Atwood family, so when she came down here, the Pratts adopted the name Atwood for Charles and Eliza. The two weren't like the other slaves. They were more accepted, like servants. The Atwoods and Pratts have always been connected in some way. My father, Pratt Atwood, worked at Continental Gin for fifty-one years.

After the Emancipation Proclamation in 1863, Atwood bought a house in the heart of Prattville. It was unusual that a former slave would have the money to purchase a home during Reconstruction and that he would move right in the middle of the white community in town. It was even more unusual that a prominent African American family would own land in Alabama as early as the 1860s. Atwood was paid so well during his servitude that not only could he afford new living quarters, but he was also one of the founding investors in Pratt's South and North Railroad. According to family beliefs, Charles Atwood is buried right outside the Pratt family cemetery, which overlooks the buildings that housed Pratt's manufacturing enterprise.

Shadrack Mims declared that his friend was generous with his slaves and provided entirely for their physical needs, buying fine clothing, erecting comfortable homes and donating a two-story building with property to the freedmen to serve as a church and day school. Many testimonials were recorded from the white townspeople about how kind Pratt's treatment was toward black slaves, but records indicate that the industrialist changed his political beliefs later in life and opposed black social equality.

Daniel Pratt's Nephew and Heir, Merrill E. Pratt

Edward Pratt became ill with consumption and, in 1835, accepted his brother Daniel's invitation to come to Alabama to improve his health. When he arrived in Prattville, Daniel informed him that he could work in the gin if he wished to and could have his choice of jobs. Edward worried about leaving his family alone in New Hampshire, however, and was especially concerned about the education of his two children, ten-year-old Augusta and seven-year-old Merrill.

After Edward passed away a few years later, his wife sent thirteen-year-old Merrill to live with his uncle in Prattville so that he might attend a good school to fulfill her husband's wishes. The two formed a close bond, and Pratt's nephew would actually grow up to become the founder's right-hand man in the gin business. Around 1860, Pratt, now in his sixties, was manufacturing about 1,500 gin stands a year, and marketing became a more complex process. He decided to hand this worry over to others and contracted with Esther's brother Samuel Ticknor and Merrill to take over the marketing of most of the gins. However, in March 1861, seven cotton states (Alabama, South Carolina, Mississippi, Florida, Georgia, Louisiana and Texas) declared their secession from the Union and joined to form the Confederate States of America. Hostilities began the next month, and the Civil War was underway. Merrill organized Company K, comprising fifty-two men, fifteen of whom probably came from his uncle's employ as mechanics and/or agents.

First Lieutenant Merrill E. Pratt, Company K, First Regiment Alabama Infantry, enrolled on March 1, 1862, and was captured at Port Hudson on July 9, 1863. He was confined with other prisoners of war at the U.S. Customs House in New Orleans, Louisiana, one of the oldest and most important federal buildings in the southern United States. It housed the U.S. Customs Service and other federal offices, but construction was suspended during the Civil War when the building was used to house captured Confederate soldiers, reportedly up to two thousand men at one time.

Merrill was finally transferred to military prison in Camp Hamilton, Virginia, on September 20, 1864, and was exchanged at Aiken's Landing, Virginia. Suffering from chronic diarrhea, he was admitted to General Hospital No. 4 in Richmond, Virginia, for a few days until his furlough and was granted leave on November 28, 1864. Merrill's military record contains a barely legible handwritten letter, dated October 24, 1864, in Prattville, from his physician attesting to his weakened condition resulting from prison confinement. The severe diarrhea could have easily been deadly, as it caused dehydration, and there really wasn't much of a cure for the disease during that time.

In addition to chronic diarrhea, combat diseases during the Civil War included mumps, measles, smallpox, influenza, malaria, typhoid, dysentery, cholera, gangrene, tuberculosis, pneumonia, yellow fever and venereal diseases. Scurvy was common due to a lack of fresh fruits and vegetables, and it was common for the soldier to experience weeks or months without bathing. To imagine each of the five human senses taxed beyond the worst conceivable nightmare would only begin to allow one to identify and depict the soldier's life. Some statistics state that one in sixty-five died in combat, one in ten was wounded and one in thirteen died from disease.

In a letter dated April 20, 1862, from Captain J.F. Whitfield to his close friend Lieutenant Merrill E. Pratt, Whitfield wrote, "Our boys stood up to the enemy like men and brave soldiers…I was very proud of them indeed." This letter was written when Captain Whitfield was taken prisoner at Camp Chase, a prison camp in Columbus, Ohio, during the Civil War. The letter was supposed to be taken to the South by Charlotte Moon Clark, a cunning spy for the Confederacy, but none of the POW letters ever left Ohio because Clark was arrested in Cincinnati on suspicion of espionage. In fact, the letters did not head south until 1948, over eighty-five years after they were written by these brave men.

By 1867, Daniel Pratt's health was failing, but he had already effectively transferred the gin factory to his capable nephew and the textile factory to Henry DeBardeleben. Merrill loved Daniel tremendously and constantly worried about his uncle's rheumatism and weakened condition.

Pratt biographer Shadrack Mims described Merrill as being a hospitable and generous person and having a big and charitable heart, especially to the poor and needy. He was born in the same New Hampshire village as his uncle, almost twenty-nine years later; attended the district school in Wilton, New Hampshire; and was sent to Prattville to continue his education and to learn the ins and outs of the business world from Daniel. Merrill married Julia Adelaide Smith, daughter of Samuel Parrish and Julia Adelaide Smith, on November 2, 1862, in Prattville. Their children were named Daniel, Mary Vaughn, Edward Samuel (died in infancy), Dora Adelaide, Julia Augusta, Henry Merrill and Merrill Eugene (died in infancy).

Daniel Pratt's estate was divided between his daughter Ellen and nephew Merrill, who bought out Ellen in 1881. Merrill not only took over the reins of operations after Daniel's death but also took over the leadership of the town and succeeded him as mayor of Prattville on May 22, 1873. He was awarded a cotton gin patent in July of that year, and the description in his own words is as follows:

My invention relates to an improvement in cotton gins; and consists in providing the sides of the hopper with circular plates, which are rotated in any suitable manner within the cotton box, the heads or sides of the box being cut away to receive the plates in such position that the inner surfaces of the heads or sides of the box correspond with the inner surfaces of the rotating plates. The plates, too, are of such a diameter and placed in such position that their circumferences cover substantially the entire surface of the

Merrill Pratt's daughter's home. *Courtesy of Rex Musgrove.*

heads or sides of the box with which the roll of cotton is likely to come in contact when the machine is in operation. The object of the invention is to diminish the friction in cotton gins of ordinary construction, caused by the roll of cotton within the hopper coming in contact with the interior surfaces of the heads or ends of the cotton box.

In short, Merrill believed that the plates would reduce friction and allow the roll to revolve more freely. A freely revolving roll would present more new surfaces to the teeth, theoretically allowing them to remove more fiber, increasing outturn whether or not they actually increased value. For over one hundred years, Merrill E. Pratt's patented gin has sat on the second floor of the gin house across the road from Old Rotation, a soil fertility experiment on the Auburn University campus in Auburn, Alabama, that began in 1896.

Neither Merrill nor his uncle saw a railroad in Prattville during their lifetimes, but one finally found its way to the city in 1895, when it was linked with the Louisville and Nashville network. Two years later, another branch line connected Prattville with the Mobile and Ohio network. Merrill continued to run the gin-manufacturing company in Prattville that became the foundation of Continental Gin Company, created in 1899, and the predecessor of the Continental Eagle Corporation.

Daniel Pratt's Son-in-Law and Protégé, Henry Fairchild DeBardeleben

Born on July 22, 1840, in Dutch Bend, a few miles from Prattville, Henry DeBardeleben was once called the "King of the Southern Iron World." His reign was the result of having the good fortune to become Daniel Pratt's ward, learning the principles of business from the great industrialist. After his father passed away, the ten-year-old DeBardeleben took a job working as an apprentice baker in a grocery store in Montgomery, Alabama, to assist his mother in paying family debts. As Daniel Pratt was a family friend, he moved to Prattville six years later and began work as a foreman in Pratt's lumberyards and cotton gin factory. By 1861, the Civil War had begun, and DeBardeleben joined the Prattville Dragoons in a fight over the secession of the Confederacy, but he resigned from the army two years later to marry Daniel Pratt's daughter.

In 1863, Henry and Ellen Pratt had tongues wagging in the small town of Prattville when they eloped in February, so much so that friends and family refused to speak to the couple after the wedding. Merrill Pratt called Ellen a willful young girl who had "had her way too long" and suspected that DeBardeleben had actually "seduced" the soon-to-be nineteen-year-old. The only two people who seemed to forgive their daughter's action were her parents, Daniel and Esther.

Pratt had come to heavily rely on his young protégé because DeBardeleben had assumed a broader responsibility in the family businesses, and they had also become close friends. In fact, DeBardeleben not only became Pratt's son-in-law but also his ward, as the industrialist taught him everything he knew about the finer points of business principles. After the War Between the States ended, Pratt began purchasing thousands of acres of land in north Alabama in order to develop coal and iron mines with DeBardeleben in mind as a partner.

Together, Pratt and DeBardeleben rebuilt the Oxmoor Furnace near Birmingham, and the latter was made the general manager of the Red Mountain Iron and Coal Company, in which Pratt held controlling interest. The Red Mountain Iron and Coal Company was the first to use ore to make pig iron during the war, even though the furnaces were destroyed during the conflict. The two men recouped their losses and reorganized the Red Mountain Iron and Coal Company as the Eureka Mining Company. The furnaces were rebuilt, and the company was reopened only a short time before Pratt died.

Henry DeBardeleben. *Courtesy of Birmingham Public Libraries.*

Joe Squire, a superintendent of the Red Mountain Company, recalled:

On May 13, 1872, Daniel Pratt and Henry F. DeBardeleben came to the Helena Mines and informed me that they had bought a controlling interest in the Red Mountain Company's mining and furnace property and requested me to keep charge of the Helena mines and also do some surveying at once at the Oxmoor furnace property. I got on their waiting train and accompanied them to Oxmoor, where they directed me to survey the boundaries of the lands, especially the Red Mountain Company's lands, and locate a mine in the Red Ore, and a tram road for the supply of the furnaces with said ore, and more especially to notify the people in the houses at the works to please vacate them as they would be needed in the course of a month for the hands.

DeBardeleben continued to be involved in the coal mining business in Jefferson County after his father-in-law's death. He was the first to succeed in making pig iron in Birmingham cheaper than that made elsewhere, built the first coal road in Alabama, induced J.W. Sloss to build furnaces, exploited the Montevallo coal fields and is credited as founding the city of Bessemer, Alabama.

Henry DeBardeleben told a *Birmingham Age-Herald* reporter when discussing his plans for Bessemer, Alabama:

> *We are going to build up a city that will contain eight furnaces within two years, and we propose to extend two railroad lines touching Tuskaloosa [sic] and another outlet to be determined. We are going to build the city solid from the bottom and establish it on a rock financial basis. It will take $100,000 for a stockholder to come in. It is thirteen miles from Birmingham, and in less than two years, the two cities will have a population of two hundred thousand. There's nothing like boring a hillside through and turning over a mountain. That's what money does, and that's what money's for. I like to use money as I use a horse—to ride! Life is one big game of poker!*

With his sons Henry and Charles, DeBardeleben explored new fields and started mining in St. Clair, Alabama, and in the Acton Basin, southeast of Birmingham. DeBardeleben was president of the Alabama Fuel and Iron Company until his death in 1910 and was connected for a time with the Birmingham Rolling Mills and the Birmingham National Bank.

Shadrack Mims, who expressed sentiments about DeBardeleben that Pratt probably would have shared, noted:

> *It absolutely strikes me with wonder and agreeable surprise how any man could accomplish so much in so short a time. It is nothing more than natural for an old man to feel proud of such an enterprising man reared up and educated in the workshops of Prattville.*

Pratt Physician, Dr. Samuel Parrish Smith and Family

Samuel Parrish Smith, the Pratt family physician and friend, was born near Clinton, Georgia, in 1814, but his father, Thomas, moved to Alabama in 1818 and was one of the early pioneers of the state. Historian Shadrack Mims stated that Thomas "was a man in whom everyone had confidence and no doubt did much good in influencing others to do right." He raised his children in a religious home, and Samuel was a shining example of his upbringing, known as a moral and charitable man and a leading member of the church.

"Prathoma." *Courtesy of Rex Musgrove.*

After Dr. Smith pursued medical studies, he settled in Prattville in 1845 in a general surgical and medical practice. The Smiths lived on a site in Prattville that would later become the future home place of Judge Eugene Thomas and the Smiths' maternal granddaughter, Julia Augusta Pratt (daughter of Merrill Edward Pratt and Julia Adelaide Smith). They named the home Prathoma.

Samuel married Adelaide Julia Allen, and six children are listed with them in the 1860 Prattville census, including Eugene, who would serve as Alabama's geologist from 1873 until his death in 1927, just short of his eighty-seventh birthday. It was he who provided the first comprehensive geological survey of the state. Eugene was one of the most respected natural scientists in the United States. Known for his small stature of five feet, four inches, he had boundless energy and determination and would visit every Alabama County in a mule-drawn wagon way before there were paved roads. It had to be an extremely bumpy ride because in his notebooks he complained about the dilapidated state of the roads.

The geologist loved exploring the countryside and never missed a chance to examine and collect geological and botanical data. He would look for minerals,

W.T. Northington home. *Courtesy of Rex Musgrove.*

which Alabama's industrialists would use to build the empire of coal, iron and steel after the Civil War. Smith photographed waterfalls, mine entrances, riverbanks and ravines to document his studies. His enormous body of work was managed at almost no pay and with very little financial support.

Eugene served in the Thirty-third Alabama Volunteers and was actually a captain on the campus of the University of Alabama in April 1865 when Federal troops burned the school. He was walking to Prattville when he found out that General Lee had surrendered and did not believe the news but met several soldiers along the way who showed him their paroles. During Alabama's reconstruction, the geologist strove to identify whatever natural resources were available to aid in the state's recovery.

Samuel and Adelaide's daughter Julia married Merrill E. Pratt, the nephew and worthy successor of Prattville industrialist and founder Daniel Pratt. The Julia A. Pratt Residence Hall of Huntingdon College in Montgomery, Alabama, is named after her because of her generosity to the institution from its beginning. In 1912, the structure was built originally as a residence for the college president, his family, faculty and students. Today, the building houses offices for student clubs and organizations.

Prominent attorney William Thomas Northington of Prattville married Julia's sister Ella in 1872. In 1882, Northington became associated with the Daniel Pratt Gin Company, and in 1887, he organized the Prattville Cotton Mills Company. Two years later, Northington organized the Continental Gin Company, of which the Daniel Pratt Gin Company is a part. He was president of this corporation from its organization in 1889 until 1903, when ill health forced him to resign.

3

BUILDING ON PRATT'S FOUNDATION

Schools

As early as 1845, Pratt had established a school for the town's children. The framed schoolhouse cost about $1,000 to erect. Pratt remembered Thomas Avery from New Hampshire as being an accomplished scholar and gentleman, so he hired him as the first teacher. By 1847, Prattville had two schools, one of which was a "ladies' school" for children. Unless employed in the mill, all of the workers' children went to the company day care center or attended Pratt's school.

In about 1860, Pratt opened the Male and Female Academy, and he served as the president on the board of trustees. The city founder spent about $9,500 in construction costs. Poet, musician and professor at John Hopkins, Sidney Lanier taught and served as principal at the academy eight years after it opened. The academy served for years as Autauga County's best school. There was a baseball team, but no football was played. Legend has it that the headmaster exclaimed, "Football is a waste of time!"

The bell at the Male and Female Academy was the work of a famous bell foundry in West Troy (now Watervliet), New York, established by Andrew Meneely, an apprentice to Julius Hanks, who started the nation's first bell foundry in 1808. These bells rang for President John Kennedy's funeral and President Lyndon Johnson's inauguration, and there are Meneely

Male and Female Academy. *Courtesy of Rex Musgrove.*

North Highland Recreation Center. *Courtesy of Alfred Wadsworth.*

bells at the Metropolitan Life building in New York City and West Point Military Academy.

Overall, the Meneely companies produced about sixty-five thousand bells. The bell at the Male and Female Academy was cast in 1859, and from that year until 1927, the town children knew its gong meant the start of classes for the day. Then, a new school was built, and the old bell was put aside until 1953, when a special tower was built to house it by the local Continental Gin Company; it still holds the bell on the school grounds today.

Daniel Pratt provided the first public school building for blacks in the Happy Hollow neighborhood. The Reverend Daniel Brown, then presiding elder of the AME church, saw the need for a junior high school and launched a movement to build the first junior high school for blacks. A site on a hill (currently Highland Park) near the Livingston home was chosen, and a three-room, two-story frame building was erected. This school was named North Highland.

In 1939, during the building program started by Superintendent Bertram King, a new facility was erected on Chestnut Street where the North Highland Headstart Center is currently located. This facility became the first high school for blacks in Prattville and the only one in the area. By 1956, a total of 191 students graduated from North Highland, and the class of 1969 was the first to graduate before the schools were desegregated.

The first public school opened its doors on September 26, 1910, after Alabama formed a board of education. Whit Moncrief, father of the current circuit clerk of Autauga County, was captain of the first undefeated Autauga County High School football team in 1938. Billy Gillespie, father of Prattville mayor Bill Gillespie, played on the 1949 and 1950 undefeated teams. The year 1974 was not a great one for football because Autauga County High went 0-10. Autauga County High School changed its name to Prattville High School in the fall of 1977.

In 2010, the school had an enrollment of 2,109 students and a faculty of 103 teachers in grades nine through twelve. Within Prattville, the public schools are Prattville Kindergarten, Daniel Pratt Elementary School (grades one through six), Prattville Primary School (grades one and two), Prattville Intermediate School (grades five and six), Prattville Junior High School (grades seven and eight), Prattville High School (grades nine through twelve) and Autauga County Technology Center.

Former city council president Dean Argo said:

My two children have gotten the very best education they could have had anywhere because, as a parent, I was always involved in the selection of

Autauga County High School. *Courtesy of Rex Musgrove.*

School parade, 1950s. *Courtesy of Rex Musgrove.*

their teachers. I never left that to the principal or the school. We were always able to choose the best teachers because we knew the teachers, went to church and socialized with them. I think Autauga County school system is very good for the limited funds that they have.

Morals, Alcohol and Religion

Elevation of the people and development of their moral characters were of the utmost concern to Daniel Pratt, especially during the early days of gin and mill operations, and he wanted his employees to have a reliable work ethic. Pratt provided the workers' families with houses of uniform size, but in each deed he required the insertion of a clause forbidding the sale of "ardent spirits" under penalty of forfeiture, and the state legislature, at his urging, prohibited the sale of liquor within two miles of the town of Prattville. "No worker about machinery is worth a pinch of salt if he has liquor in his stomach," Daniel Pratt maintained.

Pratt and his wife enjoyed glasses of fine wine during dinner, and on the hill behind his home, the city founder cultivated a vineyard of Scuppernong and Catawba grapes for his private use. He corresponded with grape growers throughout the South, discussing the best methods for improving his vineyards. One guest to Pratt's home recalled testing "several specimens of fine Autauga wine." But temperance—meaning total abstinence from alcoholic liquors—was one of Pratt's major concerns when it came to his employees and, in general, the citizens of his town. This was also a concern of the Prattville Bible Society, which had organized by 1846. Distribution of Bibles to indigent families was the group's primary goal.

Daniel Pratt noted, "The town's inhabitants are industrious, intelligent and refined, and the town is universally free of the vices of loafing and dissipation."

Pratt was described as a true Christian man, greatly interested in offering his employees many educational and religious advantages. To this end, Pratt put up a temporary place for a house of worship in the upper room of a two-story building, which was fitted for seats, and told his sister in a letter that he was proud his village had decent churches and schools:

Should my life be spared a few years longer, I think I shall accomplish what I have been striving for. That is, build up a respectable village such as will compare with your Northern towns in point of good morals and good society. We have regular preaching every Sabbath and generally every Wednesday night, and I think as good as you have in Milford. We have a Methodist Church numbering one hundred or more members, a respectable Baptist Church and Presbyterian. We also have an excellent school the year round besides a ladies school for small children. We have a Sabbath school numbering one hundred and twenty scholars. We also have a Bible class.

Currently, according to the Church Angel directory database, there are about ninety-three churches within the city limits of Prattville.

Methodist

In his religious views, Mr. Pratt was a Methodist both in heart and practice. He was not merely a nominal member of the church, but one who enjoyed his religion.
—Shadrack Mims

Esther Pratt, originally a Presbyterian, converted to Methodism along with her husband in 1832. The town founder helped to organize the Methodist Church around 1844, outfitting the upper room of a store near Autauga Creek to serve as a place of worship. In addition to the Pratts, the surviving register, kept by recording steward and physician Samuel Parrish Smith, shows that a wide spectrum of townspeople belonged to the congregation in the 1850s. There were Shadrack Mims, Samuel Parrish Smith and those who served as church stewards, including physician Hugh Hillhouse, attorney Thomas Sadler, merchant Benjamin Miles, bookkeeper William Ormsby, clerk Norman Cameron, shop owners Thomas Ormsby and James Wainwright and mechanic James Tunnell.

By 1852, the church claimed 251 members, and the small room above Benjamin Miles's store was getting cramped. Pratt spent $20,000 of his own money to construct a new church from his own design and called it no less than "probably the best brick building in Alabama." The church has been in a couple of different sites in the downtown area but celebrated its 100th anniversary of worship in its current location in May 2012.

Methodist Church Pratt built. *Courtesy of Rex Musgrove.*

First United Methodist Church. *Courtesy of Alfred Wadsworth.*

According to the 1849 *Southern Statesman*, "Good morals and well paid industry distinguish the operatives. The religious program for Pratt's workers represents a model for the guidance of every community."

Presbyterian

In 1846, the First Presbyterian Church of Prattville was organized and first located near the cotton gin factory on the south side of Autauga Creek on Bridge Street. That original building is now located on Sixth Street, the property of First Missionary Baptist Church.

During the tenure of Pastor James K. Hazen (1861–77), who married Mary Ticknor, niece of town founder Daniel Pratt, poet Sidney Lanier served as the church organist. Hazen, a former classmate of James A. Garfield, the twentieth president of the United States, was elected secretary of publication by the General Assembly of the Presbyterian Church. The second structure, a Victorian-style building, was built and furnished in 1896 at the present location.

Just after the beginning of World War II in January 1941, the sanctuary was destroyed by fire. The *Prattville Progress* headline read: "Last Wednesday night, Prattville suffered a tremendous loss when the First Presbyterian Church was totally destroyed by fire. Two old pianos and a few chairs were all that was saved."

Gene Kerlin, Prattaugan Museum volunteer, recalled, "I was ten years old in January of 1941 when the wooden Presbyterian Church burned. I lived on Wetumpka Street, and we could see the fire from on top of the hill."

A new facility was constructed later in 1941. Several additions were made in the 1950s and 1960s. In 1982, the Gordon Musgrove family commissioned the Vertian Company of Atlanta, Georgia, to forge a brass bell that is still rung today. A new sanctuary was constructed in 2008 after cracks in the structure developed due to unpredictable soil. The most radical change was moving the entrance from South Chestnut Street to West Third.

Left: Original Presbyterian Church. *Courtesy of Rex Musgrove.*

Below: First Presbyterian Church. *Courtesy of Rex Musgrove.*

Baptist

Even though Pratt was a Methodist, he openly encouraged his employees to attend a church of their choice. By 1846, Prattville had Baptist, Methodist and Presbyterian churches, all of which were located near the western side of Autauga Creek on land donated by Pratt. Large numbers of mill families were able to join a Sunday service of their choice. The Reverend G.W. Molett was the first pastor of First Baptist Church, originally organized as the Unity Missionary Baptist Church in 1838.

The church membership grew so much that a larger building was needed. In October 1840, Pratt deeded land on the western side of Autauga Creek to the church, and a new building, approximately thirty feet by forty-four feet, was constructed. Economic hardships drew more people to the church during the Reconstruction period, and membership grew from 54 to 220. The church began to hold weekly prayer meetings every night. During Alexander Sims's six years as pastor at Unity, the church built a new house of worship.

Old Baptist Church. *Courtesy of Rex Musgrove.*

In 1899, the church moved into its new building and was called Prattville Baptist Church. The attendance kept growing in the early 1900s to over four hundred members. In the late 1930s, the church began broadcasting its morning service over WCOV television in the nearby city of Montgomery. The one-hour broadcast cost $1.50. In 1947, the church voted to rename itself First Baptist Church of Prattville; continued growth dictated yet another expansion a few years later, and a new building was erected in 1954.

Episcopal

One of my cousins of both parents and my fourth grade teacher, Erin Chapman, designed St. Mark's Episcopal Church and played the organ there. She was my third or fourth cousin on both sides. My grandfather, H.D. Murphree, was a foreman at the gin shop.
—Susan Cranfield

St. Mark's Episcopal Church was formally organized in 1859 and was admitted to the Episcopal Diocese of Alabama in 1877. Services were first held at the Presbyterian church and in the old courthouse. In 1876, a white wood-frame chapel was purchased from the Methodists. It was moved from the south side of Autauga Creek near the gin factory to near the church's current location on East Fourth Street and was last used as a schoolroom for the local high school's senior class in 1910.

The present Gothic revival church was erected in 1909. It was not the first church built in Prattville, but it is the oldest standing church in the city. A longtime organist at the church, Erin Chapman, who was also a fourth-grade teacher for many years at Prattville Primary School, partially designed the building when she was sixteen years old. The small parish house west of the nave was built in 1953 and enlarged in 1966 and 1984. It is named in honor of the Chapman family.

St. Mark's Episcopal Church. *Courtesy of Rex Musgrove.*

Early Businesses

In 1846, when I moved here, there had been but few buildings put up. There was one where John Hearn lived, two between that and Joe Hurd's drugstore. I do not know who occupied this house, but think it was Amos Smith, the father of G.L. Smith. There was also a building built by Joseph May from whom Mr. Pratt bought 1,000 acres of land and the water privilege, paying him $20,000—one half in gins at factory prices. I settled where F.E. Smith now lives, and that has been one of the healthiest places in Prattville, water very cool, pure and abundant. A tinner by the name of George H. Tisdale built the house, which is now the Methodist parsonage. Col. L.G. Spigner came here very soon after its first settlement, perhaps in 1840. He was engaged in the business of wagon making and repairing and had a blacksmith's shop.
—Shadrack Mims

In the 1850s, Prattville contained a textile mill; a woolen mill; gristmills; a sash, door and blind manufactory; and a foundry. The town had about six mercantile stores. W.C. Allen and Company, owned by New York natives W.C. Allen and his brother Hassan, was a popular establishment and sold clothing, jewelry, hardware, tobacco, toys and books, just to name a few, and advertised all items "at the lowest prices."

In addition to the merchants, Prattville also had six physicians, three attorneys, six teachers and eight men employed in building trades. Travelers to the city in the 1850s could stay at the Tennessee House and Stables and dine at Casimir and Jacob Krout's restaurant. Prattville's middle class in the 1850s included most of the town's merchants; all its physicians and attorneys; teachers William Miles and Jere S. Williams; agent Shadrack Mims; shop owners William Clepper, James Wainwright, David Suter and Llewellyn Spigner; and such highly skilled mechanics as Nathan Morris, Harris Ware, Joshua White and B. W. Rogers.

The Prattville Mercantile was built in 1855 by Daniel Pratt to serve as his company's store and housed offices for his businesses. The building survived the 1900 fire that destroyed most of downtown Prattville, and the first bank was also housed there. Joseph Bell, who married Mary Pratt, daughter of Daniel's nephew Merrill, remained employed at the store for many years from the early 1900s. Prior to his employment at the store, in 1890, Bell served as manager of the order department for the Daniel Pratt Gin Company.

Prattville Mercantile. *Courtesy of Rex Musgrove.*

In Prattville, there were three druggists, a dentist, a shoemaker and fourteen merchants in 1860. A druggist, Joseph Hurd, sold such items as toilet water, makeup, cigars, Moffat's Life Pills and Phoenix Butter, while his competitor, Spong and Root, boasted butter and soda crackers fresh from the bakery, valentines, perfume and a soda joint. The town had two boardinghouses run by widows of shop owners and a lively oyster saloon that sold oysters, whiskey, brandy, ale, champagne, wines, tobacco, cigars and snuff.

Daniel Pratt advocated shopping local long before the modern locavore movement:

> *Instead of these angry debates at our public meetings, let us unite and say we will give Southern manufacturers the preference. If all would unite in this plan and carry it out, it would not be long before they could be supplied at home with most of the articles we consume, and such as are not made here, our own merchants could import.*

Thomas Ormsby and George Smith ran a machine shop that serviced Pratt's factories. Enoch Robinson made horse mills, and Ephraim Morgan made sashes, doors and blinds in shops that were next to Pratt's factories.

Cannon's five-and-ten store. *Courtesy of Rex Musgrove.*

J.T. Weeks Repair Shop. *Courtesy of Rex Musgrove.*

William Bush served as the town's dentist, and Jay DeWitt Wheat was employed as a bookkeeper. The town's first newspaper editors were William Howell and T.S. Luckett, who started the *Autauga Citizen* with financial help from Daniel Pratt. Howell and Luckett immediately made the *Citizen* a platform for the views of Pratt and like-minded Prattville boosters:

> *If the South, with all its advantages in natural resources would only follow Prattville's example and turn its energies to diversified pursuits, she would soon occupy a position to be envied by the first nationals of the earth in point of commercial greatness. Without the South's abundant natural riches, both England and New England had become major industrial centers. Moreover, manufacturing would benefit the South socially as well as economically by giving employment to thousands of the region's young men who might otherwise drag out a miserable existence in idleness and profligacy. If only the true sentiments concerning the respectability of labor were instilled in the minds of these idle young men, they could be profitably employed as shop mechanics and factory superintendents and overseers, just as in Prattville.*

First Courthouse

The Autauga County seat was moved from Kingston to Prattville in 1868. Located on Court Street directly across from the creek and gin complex, the first courthouse in Prattville was built in 1870 with the designs of local architect and early pioneer George Littlefield Smith, occupant of the McWilliams-Smith-Rice House (presently the Prattaugan Museum). The two-story brick building had a gabled roof and wide eaves supported by paired scrolled brackets. It is a perfect example of the Italianate style of architecture. The courtroom was on the second floor, and the jail was located behind the structure. If you look high above the front entrance, you can see "Courthouse 1870."

This courthouse and jail sold for $5,000 around 1905, and the money from the sale aided in erecting a new building. A Romanesque revival courthouse was designed by the firm of Bruce Architectural Company of Birmingham and built in 1906. It replaced the county's 1870 courthouse, which still stands a bit to the north of the new structure.

Courthouse. *Courtesy of Rex Musgrove.*

Railroad

The South and North Railroad bypassed Prattville, running about eight miles east of town. Pratt and the town's most prominent citizens met at the county courthouse to discuss the matter in December 1871. A five-man committee was chosen to speak with the president and directors of the South and North Railroad. Pratt, state senator James Farden, Democratic attorneys William H. Northington and Henry J. Livingston and Republican planter and former attorney John L. Alexander made up the committee.

The committee reported to a large crowd assembled at the courthouse, and Northington offered a resolution that Prattville should raise the money for a branch road to the South and North by imposing a direct tax, which the assembly unanimously adopted. More committees were then chosen to petition the legislature to authorize the town council to levy a special railroad tax to raise the money for a branch railroad and to solicit Montgomery's board of trade for aid in building the road.

Early 1900s. *Courtesy of Rex Musgrove.*

The *Alabama State Journal* suggested that Montgomery and Prattville work together in bringing the railroad to Prattville because both locations would benefit from the branch line. The railroad bill passed so that the council could impose the tax, and Prattvillians bought railroad stock subscriptions, with $50,000 coming from the town and $50,000 from its founder, $20,000 from Merrill Pratt and $20,000 from Henry DeBardeleben. Altogether, twenty-five men (excluding the Pratts and DeBardeleben) had committed a total of $10,400 to the project.

However, even with this large commitment of financial resources, the railroad project failed, perhaps because Montgomery investors were not as forthcoming as Prattvillians had hoped due to other local matters that needed financial backing. Pratt had become involved in the takeover of the Red Mountain Iron and Coal Company during this same time, so perhaps he found himself short of capital. Nevertheless, the next couple of years saw a severe economic depression in both Europe and the United States and in Daniel Pratt's death; both of these events undermined further attempts to construct the road in the 1870s. In fact, Prattville was not able to get the railroad until 1895.

4

A CITY AND A NATION IN CRISIS

Before the Civil War

Practically before Daniel Pratt's very eyes, his town expanded into a major manufacturing and marketing center a few years prior to the Civil War. His enterprises continued to prosper and so did the town. The citizens wanted a railroad, charitable organizations were organized and more emphasis was placed on the establishment of churches and schools. Statewide, Alabama's twenty-four cotton factories were running more than 100,000 spindles—over 1,000 looms—with an investment of $2 to $3 million and giving employment to three thousand Negro slaves and poor whites. This was an excellent example of the growing diversification of Alabama's antebellum economy.

Pratt was proud to say that his town had good morals and family values, but even the most saintly of societies have small lapses where fighting would break out in the open spaces of city streets, and Prattville was no exception in the early days. At any rate, those incidents only infrequently acted to provide entertainment for the citizens. Afterward, the city would revert back to the sleepy, tranquil "good" society about which Pratt always dreamed.

In his vision, Pratt sought for Prattville to be much more than just a company town, and since the population grew from 448 to 943 between 1850 and 1860, Pratt encouraged new businesses by renting factory space to enterprising mechanics. He liquidated his own company store so that merchants could begin their own businesses. New merchants doubled over that ten-year period, and Prattville became more than just a factory town.

The War Between the States

The reasons for the Civil War have been widely debated by people for many years. In addition to the slavery issue, the most important causes Southerners listed for the war were unfair taxation and states' rights—or the right to govern themselves as an independent nation. There were two very different economies at play because the North made money from factories and manufacturing while the South relied on agriculture for its main income. The government collected duties on the agricultural products exported to Britain by the South and on the manufactured goods the South imported from Britain. The South actually kept the federal government solvent. Not only did these unfair taxes anger the Southerners, but also the revenue garnered from them was expended more in the North than in the South.

It is also supposed that the cause of states' rights was tied in closely with the South feeling that the federal government should not interfere with slavery in those states where it already existed. Northerners felt that slavery was morally wrong, but it continued to flourish in the plantation economy of the South. In Alabama, the slave-owning planters were dominant because of the prosperous cotton crop, and as the Civil War loomed closer, the support of Southern rights and secession grew. Whether slavery in the South would have faded away without cotton production is unknown, but it may have altered the development of sectional conflict before 1861.

Alabama seceded from the Union on January 11, 1861. Women in Montgomery presented to the secession convention a flag bearing a single star. The following month, delegates from six other seceded states met in Montgomery to create the new government of the Confederate States of America.

Jefferson Davis, after resigning from the United States Senate, was selected to be the provisional president of the Confederate States and took oath on February 18, 1861, in Montgomery, which was serving as the first capital of the Confederacy. Pratt was opposed to secession in the beginning because he had no confidence the South could sustain itself without the help of the North, but once Alabama had withdrawn from the Union, he was "all in," so to speak, and fully supported his state in the upcoming conflict.

The war was imminent, and there was much consternation and worry among the Autauga County citizens. They wondered whether the native sons should enlist in some branch of the military to protect the Southern homeland, but a man named Samuel D. Oliver from a neighboring community eased their fears and gave them the idea to form a local company. He urged the necessity of organizing a military unit and met with George Littlefield Smith, a prominent Prattville builder, at his home in Prattville to convey those sentiments.

After this meeting, a group of volunteers met at Alida Hall, the large upper room of Daniel Pratt's cotton gin factory, and formed the Prattville Guards, with Oliver as captain. The company was registered by the state adjutant general as part of the Alabama Volunteer Corps, putting it on a special list of commands that could be called into active military service at any time, and it was the first Autauga County Unit to volunteer in the struggle for Southern rights. Within a few months, members decided to change the name and reorganize for mounted service; thus, the Prattville Dragoons were born.

On April 11, 1861, the order to fire on Fort Sumter, the act that started the Civil War, was sent from a downtown building serving as the telegraph office in Montgomery. Because the Confederate capital was moved to Richmond, Virginia, in May, Montgomery remained virtually untouched by conflict during the war. However, at the end of the war in April 1865, General James Wilson's federal raiders entered the city. Local citizens burned more than 100,000 bales of cotton to prevent it falling into Union hands. As far as Prattville herself, the war left the city and the county virtually unscathed, as no battles were fought on Autauga County soil.

Former Continental Eagle employee and historian Tommy Brown noted:

> *I've gotten this story from several sources. When Pratt heard the Yankees were coming in toward Selma, he went up to Breakfast Creek, a few miles north of the city at that time, with a wagon full of guns. He said, "This is all we have in town." The Yankees went on to Selma and avoided Prattville.*

Selma, Alabama, housed an industrial complex that produced nearly all the war materials for the Confederate troops near the end of the Civil War. The 6.4 Brooke cannon, weighing more than ten thousand pounds, was produced there, as were different types of musket bullets and Colt round balls. The gunboats *Gaines*, *Selma* and *Morgan* were built and outfitted in Selma, and almost every item needed by the Confederate soldiers in the field was manufactured there.

On April 2, 1865, General James H. Wilson's Federal troops captured the city and completely destroyed the arsenal, ordnance center, gunpowder works, ironworks and foundries. Just about a week after the Battle of Selma, General Robert E. Lee surrendered the Army of Northern Virginia to General Ulysses S. Grant at Appomattox Courthouse, Virginia, and the war was effectively over. The total casualty count that is most often quoted is 620,000.

Prattville Dragoons

Many not being able to furnish their mounts were greatly discouraged. That great and good man, Daniel Pratt, so well known for deeds of charity and generosity, supplied the deficiency at a cost of many hundred dollars.
—*Captain W.F. Mims, Prattville Dragoons, in* War History of the Prattville Dragoons

As the men were being organized, many did not have horses and were greatly discouraged on joining the fight. Pratt rode to the rescue and, using his own money, purchased the mounts, in addition to contributing to the support of the volunteers' families. About twenty-five of the Prattville Academy students with an average age of sixteen joined the company, and twelve Pratt employees enlisted, including Henry DeBardeleben. Fourteen of the brave young students were killed, and seven were wounded.

The town founder presented to each dragoon member a uniform made of black broadcloth trimmed with gold braid. Women of the town made the silk flag, which was presented to the company at the time of its sendoff by Miss Abbie Holt, daughter of Pratt's sister, at the Male and Female Academy in 1861.

The first captain of the dragoons was Jesse Cox from Mobile, one of the most famous steamboat captains on the Alabama River. An interesting sidebar is that the citizens of Montgomery, Alabama, presented Cox with a large silver water cooler in 1858. Thought to have been buried by the slaves of Captain Cox to prevent its being stolen by Wilson's Federal Raiders in April 1865, the water cooler was given to the First White House of the Confederacy in Montgomery in the 1930s by Cox's granddaughter, M. Otis Cox of Connecticut.

In total, there were originally eighteen commissioned and noncommissioned officers and eighty-two privates, with two faithful black cooks. During the first couple years, many of the soldiers in the Confederate army had their own Negro servants in the field with them who waited on their masters, cleaned their horses and cooked their meals. Later on, as the service got much harder and rations became scarcer, the servants were sent back home, and the men did their own work.

The unit was sent to Pensacola, Florida, to become part of General Bragg's army and camped for ten months on the bay training to be fighting soldiers. The next stop was Chattanooga, Tennessee, where the men participated in the Battle of Shiloh in 1862. By January 1864, they had received no pay for services for six months, and their clothing was so ragged that it did not warm their bodies during the severe winters. Some were even without shoes, few had overcoats and many were without tents, and they marched and slept in snow and rain. The dragoons bravely fought in many battles, suffering many casualties along the way, and finally, reduced to virtually a skeleton army, they surrendered in North Carolina as part of General Joseph E. Johnston's surrender on April 26, 1865. They disbanded and returned to their homes.

In 1916, the United Daughters of the Confederacy placed a large boulder with a bronze plaque at the schoolyard of the Prattville Academy to honor the dragoons. It reads:

> *This boulder is erected by the Merrill E. Pratt Chapter U.D.C. April 26, 1916 marks the spot where the Prattville Dragoons assembled in April 1861 on the eve of their departure to the war and is commemorative of their patriotism in the Confederate service.*

Reconstruction

When the Confederate armies surrendered after four bloody years of war, the South needed to rebuild and re-form politically, economically and socially. Even before the end of the war, President Abraham

Lincoln issued the Emancipation Proclamation to free the slaves in the Confederate states involved in the rebellion, but the executive order itself did not outlaw slavery and did not make the ex-slaves citizens. Therefore, the president pushed for the passage of the Thirteenth Amendment to the United States Constitution, which was finally adopted on December 6, 1865, some eight months after he was assassinated by John Wilkes Booth. On that date, all remaining slaves (who were not freed following the end of the war) became officially free men, or "freedmen." Now, the country was faced with the challenge of bringing the states back together as one nation, socially and economically.

The Civil War struck hard at all manufacturers, and Pratt faced just as many hardships as the rest of the Southern businessmen. Simply put, the mill machinery fell apart as the conflict raged. Pratt said that it was next to impossible to build good machinery, and consequently no one could do good work. He could not collect payments from ruined planters who had bought gins before the conflict had started. In 1871, Pratt's lawyers asserted that war-related losses to his gin business amounted to nearly $405,000. Simply put, both the founder's businesses *and* his town suffered immensely during the war.

Cash was in short supply. Stores lay empty. Goods and essentials were cut off by the Northern blockade, and industry withered. Plantations and factories closed all over the South. Mills located in the Tennessee Valley were all wantonly destroyed in 1862 and 1863. Cotton gin sales declined. The mill in Prattville suffered much damage during the war but was rebuilt. Following the war, Autauga County's population dropped to 11,623 in 1870 from 16,739 in 1860. Shadrack Mims recalled:

> *I was called to the position of cotton mill Agent in January 1865. I made a statement of the business as it then stood. There were about 700 bales of cotton on hand, but the whole machinery, having worked steadily for four years, was worn down and could not compete, either in quality or quantity of cloth, with mills that were in better condition. I so notified the managers and further said there were only two alternatives before them, stop the mill, sell the cotton and divide out the proceeds; or fill the mill with new machinery. My opinion was that the latter would be the most profitable to the stockholders. But, there were two things that troubled Mr. Pratt; what would become of the operatives, and one of his darling projects would have to be abandoned. Mr. Pratt was president of the Board, and the other managers yielded to his wishes. New machines having been ordered, the mill*

continued to run, and the old machinery worked up all the cotton, and the goods were sold at reduced rates.

Pratt saw the need to further aid in Prattville's recovery during the Reconstruction period and was able to call in some debts with Northern accounts. This enabled him to rebuild his own operations and, in turn, help Autauga County through this financial crisis. He pursued old debtors and beckoned new customers. Pratt also built a four-mile-long plank road at a cost of several thousand dollars from his plant to Washington Landing on the Alabama River in order to aid in delivering gin stands that were being transported by steamboat. In 1866, he placed a fresh advertisement for his gins in *De Bow's Review*, proclaiming that his factory was back in operation.

These are just a few examples of how the founding father deeply cared about the citizens of Prattville. From a business and financial standpoint, it probably would have behooved him to cease the mill operations and sell the cotton just to salvage whatever was left of the factory, but Pratt was too concerned about his employees being left without jobs and unable to feed and clothe their families. An early advocate of "buy at home," the industrial giant encouraged trade within the state and within the South itself.

Daniel Pratt wrote in the *Montgomery Journal*:

> *Let us show a disposition to encourage home industry and home trade. Instead of going to New York and Boston for almost everything we consume, let us encourage our own tailors, shoemakers, tanners, saddlers, cabinet makers, pail makers, broom makers, cotton gin makers, cotton and woolen factories and many other branches of business. It may be said we have no good tailors, shoemakers, etc., but should we show a disposition to encourage those various branches. We soon would have mechanics among us and as good and cheap a coat made here as we can get from New York, and so with all other branches. Could not our merchants be supplied in Charleston, Savannah, Mobile and New Orleans instead of going to New York? When this shall take place, then we shall be in a much better condition to secede. Then, the abolition chord will be loosened. Then, we shall be a prosperous and happy people.*

5

COTTON GIN MANUFACTURING
AFTER DANIEL PRATT

Merrill Pratt's Reign

While Daniel Pratt's son-in-law, the wild and daring Henry DeBardeleben, concentrated on mineral land in Jefferson County, Alabama, Pratt's nephew Merrill continued to focus completely on Prattville. He solely owned the business after falling heir to half Pratt's estate and buying out Ellen DeBardeleben's share, which she gained after her father's death.

The gin factory continued to prosper with Merrill at the helm. These gins were used in every cotton-growing region on earth. Over one hundred of them were sent to Russia in 1891. In 1898, twenty-five years after Daniel Pratt's death, the gin factory made 1,500 gins annually, and the cotton mill produced eighteen to twenty-two thousand yards of cloth per day. Both mill buildings had three hundred looms and ten thousand spindles and were equipped with an electric plant with 430 incandescent lights.

After a freshet destroyed the cotton mill in 1886, Merrill helped form the Prattville Cotton Mills and Banking Company, which quickly rebuilt the factory building and filled it with machinery. The next year, the company added more machinery and an additional building. Original stockholders of the company included Merrill and his oldest son Daniel, Lafayette Ellis, Charles Doster and William T. Northington. Northington married Ella Smith, making him a son-in-law of Samuel Parrish Smith

Gin complex. *Courtesy of Marc Parker.*

and a brother-in-law to Merrill. Upon Merrill Pratt's death in 1889, employees at the gin factory once again answered to a man named Daniel Pratt.

Merrill E. Pratt's obituary in the *Prattville Progress* on November 29, 1889, read:

> *We never had a sadder duty to perform than to chronicle the death of our beloved townsman and foremost citizen, Hon. Merrill E. Pratt, which sad event occurred at his residence in Prattville last Saturday morning. He was confined to his bed not more than a week with pneumonia. Mr. Pratt was born in Temple, New Hampshire, February 23, 1828, and came to Alabama when twelve years of age, casting his lot in this lovely village, which his famous uncle, the lamented Daniel Pratt, had founded a few years before. He served as First Lieutenant of Company K, 1st Alabama Regiment, in the late war. He was unanimously elected two years ago to the general assembly where he made a faithful representative of the state and county. The deceased leaves behind a most estimable wife, two sons and three daughters.*

Daniel Pratt II and More Mergers

After Merrill Pratt passed away in 1889, the town's destiny fell upon his son Daniel Pratt II, who was also treasurer and afterward president of the Prattville Cotton Mills & Banking Company and treasurer of the Northington-Munger-Pratt company of Birmingham until the absorption of this company by the Continental Gin Company. The Daniel Pratt Cotton Gin Company merged with other manufacturers in 1899 to form the Continental Gin Company, which was headquartered in Birmingham. With the expertise of different companies, the manufacture of cotton gins progressed to a science.

In the early 1900s, Continental Gin limited itself to two styles of elevators, built additional warehouse space and consolidated its manufacturing efforts. Continental began diversification into other fields of manufacture prior to 1940, and then during World War II this diversification was well tested when production was almost exclusively devoted to producing materials for the armed forces.

Daniel Pratt Jr. was born on February 12, 1866, in Prattville, attended schools in the city and graduated from the University of Alabama in 1885. In addition to his responsibilities at Continental Gin, Merrill's son was elected president of the Autauga Banking and Trust Company, was a city council member and served as a member of the board of trustees of the University of Alabama. He married Ellen, a daughter of Leonard and Sallie Sims of Prattville. They had five children: Merrill Edward, Leonard Sims, Dora Ellen, Julia and Jennie Allyn. An interesting piece of trivia is that in every generation of the core Pratt families, there was named a Merrill and a Daniel. Merrill's oldest son died at the ripe old age of eighty-three years.

The *Anniston Star* of October 28, 1949, reported:

> *While friends and admirers of the late Daniel Pratt, Jr. are legion throughout Alabama and the South, it is doubtful that there is anyone better qualified than Cash Stanley to eulogize the noble Alabamian whose death was reported in the* Alabama Journal *of Montgomery. Mr. Stanley has this to say about his late friend with whom he was long and closely associated with: "The death of Daniel Pratt, Jr. in Prattville at the age of 83 severs another of the powerful links in Alabama which bind the distant past with the teeming present. Daniel Pratt, Jr. was a nephew of the original Daniel Pratt who founded the city of Prattville in the 1800s*

and made it a center of great industry. Daniel Pratt, Jr. succeeded to his uncle's established business in Prattville and branched out extensively in commerce and banking until he became himself a tower of business strength in his community and state."

Fulton Industries of Atlanta acquired controlling interest of the company in April 1959. This company emphasized company and facility growth, and production changed to all-electric power. Fulton consolidated production from Birmingham and Dallas to the Prattville plant and relocated its offices to Prattville. Some older buildings, including the lumber house, dry kiln and Daniel Pratt's home were destroyed and replaced with a 118,000-square-foot steel and masonry facility, which brought the complex to more than 450,000 square feet of office, plant and warehouses. Operations moved from the nineteenth-century buildings to a single-floor factory.

The following is an ad in the *Prattville Progress* displayed on July 21, 1960:

Continental Gin in Record Year of Total Sales. Continental Gin Company Birmingham World's Largest Manufacturer of Complete Cotton Ginning systems is Experiencing a Record Year of Sales Thus Far in 1960.

In 1962, the Continental Gin Company moved its headquarters from Birmingham to Prattville, and two years later, a merger brought together Continental with Moss-Gordin Company. This was the perfect opportunity and method to accomplish accelerated expansion quickly and efficiently. Continental/Moss-Gordin introduced its 93-saw and 141-saw gin stands around 1973. The gins used sixteen-inch-diameter saws and were rated at five and seven and a half bales per hour, respectively. Features of these gins included dual moting, stainless steel roll box, top-mounted ginning ribs and doffing brushes. In 1986, that firm was consolidated with Murray-Carver, Inc., to form Continental Eagle Corporation.

If the above information and many name changes are bewildering and confusing, Tommy Brown should be thanked for the following simple breakdown: Daniel Pratt Gin Company (1832–1850), Samuel Griswold & Company (a short-lived partnership, 1850–1853), Daniel Pratt Gin Company (1853–1899), Continental Gin Company (1899–1964), Continental/Moss-Gordin Company (1964–1975), Bush Hog/Continental Gin (1975–1986) and Continental Eagle Corporation (1986–2012).

Continental Eagle Corporation

David Mrozinski, former vice-president of international sales at Continental Eagle Corporation, stated:

> *We supply cotton-ginning equipment anywhere in the world. About 65 percent of our business was international over the last fifteen years. Prior to that, we were probably 24 to 35 percent international, and the rest was domestic. Our domestic market has been diminishing. It's being picked up in other parts of the world. Cotton production is actually going up worldwide, so there's still a need for it, but there are more and more machine manufacturers that are coming up in developing countries, so they are cutting into our pie. We're getting more and more competition overseas.*

Employee Tommy Brown recalled:

> *When I first got into the business some twenty-five years or so ago, I'd go down to the cotton press pit. How the machinery worked just awed me. Six hundred tons of force packing bails continuously is just amazing.*

It was a full manufacturing facility, so there were sheet metal workers, machinists and welders—very high-quality craftsmen. Some of the older equipment with castings was very precise. Steel castings date back to the Daniel Pratt days. They were sort of a combination of cast steel and wood from the late 1800s, and samples could be found in Continental Eagle's R&D facility. Gun turrets for ships were made there. During World War II, employees worked on the Manhattan Project, but they didn't know they were working on bombs.

According to Rachel Deaile in the *Montgomery Advertiser*:

> *Actually it was bomb casings for chemical and fragment bombs, spinners and naval gun mounts. The Gin Company had an office in Washington, D.C. for the duration of World War II. Recently, some of these bomb casings were found in the Gin Shop basement in a hole in the wall and are on display at the Prattaugan Museum and Visitor Center in downtown Prattville.*

Continental Eagle grew well until the mid-1990s, and there were about four hundred employees in 1993. It had seven locations in the United States that were sales and service, some minor manufacturing and re-wrapping saws and refurbishing components for the local markets. Continental Eagle was the largest producer of cotton ginning equipment in the world and the oldest continuously operated industrial complex in Alabama, dating to the founding of the Daniel Pratt Gin Company; however, on January 12, 2012, it ceased operations, and all employees were permanently laid off.

This announcement came on the heels of phasing out the manufacture of cotton gins and related machinery in the Prattville plant in 2009 due to the extended downturn in the cotton industry in the United States and throughout the cotton-growing regions of the world combined with significant raw material cost increases. Light manufacturing was retained at the company for repairs for a small number of items.

In essence, the company primarily operated for a couple years as a marketing and engineering firm, maintaining expertise in machinery and system design and distribution of products to the cotton industry. The manufacture of nearly the entire product line was transferred to Bajaj Steel Industries, Ltd., a highly respected manufacturer of cotton gin machinery in Nagpur, India. The following is former mayor Jim Byard Jr.'s reaction to the 2009 announcement of downsizing at Continental Eagle:

In 1988, there were approximately 1,600 cotton gins in America, while today, just over twenty years later, there are just over 700 gins. Due to technological advancements, more cotton is ginned today by fifty percent less gins. Last year, cotton producing acreage in our country decreased by an estimated fifty percent. This information clearly illustrates what the management of Continental has struggled to overcome in an effort to stay afloat. I am confident that today's announcement [December 15, 2009] *will allow the legacy and the company that our founder Daniel Pratt started in 1832 to remain the same. Further, it allows the company's family ownership to remain the same and positions Continental Eagle to continue meeting the needs of their customers.*

After Continental Eagle ceased operations, rumors circulated throughout the city that the historic buildings dating all the way back to the time of Prattville's founder were to be razed and used for salvage. But, the rumors were only partially correct, as there were potential buyers interested in the property for development, and one such developer is eyeing the buildings for residential use. According to the *Athens Banner-Herald*:

A Brief History of the Fountain City

A Georgia company hopes to transform the historic mill in Prattville into a downtown attraction that includes dozens of loft apartments. Burke Lambert, a principal with Atlanta-based Longstreet Capitol, says the mill property is one of the last of its types in the nation that hasn't been developed for another purpose. Lambert tells the Montgomery Advertiser *that he envisions sweeping green spaces, stunning views of the mill pond and a hundred and sixty loft apartments. He said the historic brick buildings are in remarkably good shape. The thirty-acre property includes about a dozen buildings. The sale of the property is dependent on the city rezoning the land from business to residential use.*

The request to rezone was filed by Lambert, a representative for Pratt Mill Partners, LLC, and the Prattville City Council approved the rezoning request for the town's historic cotton gin mill in June 2012. The Autauga County Heritage Association has spent a great deal of time and effort moving and safeguarding the contents of the Continental Eagle Gin Company so that the history of Daniel Pratt and the town he built remains in Prattville. Some of these items and many more historical artifacts can be viewed at the Prattaugan Museum on East Main Street.

Mayor Bill Gillespie Jr. noted:

This endeavor will be very beneficial to the city of Prattville, as well as Autauga County. We look forward to the future development of this property, which should showcase these historic buildings making much the same impact as was made when our fair city was built around them. The timing couldn't be more opportune for historic downtown and the citizens of Prattville.

6

RECOLLECTIONS OF A GROWING CITY

Whit Moncrief

B.W. Moncrief general store has been a permanent fixture in Prattville since the early 1900s. The family's roots are imbedded deeply into the city, and the store is the true definition of a family business, with four generations of Moncriefs employed there in some way or another through the years. Whit Moncrief, the current Autauga County circuit clerk, is the great grandson of the man whose name (B.W. Moncrief) is printed high on the old building and the person who is so familiar with its operation because he "grew up" in the store. His grandfather was W.H. "Hollie" Moncrief, his father was called "Whit" and he was nicknamed "Lil (or Little) Whit."

Whit Moncrief recalled:

> *We started in 1900 across the street, but in 1910, we built the present building where we are now and sold groceries up to 1939. They called it a dry goods store, but we sold clothing, some furniture and some appliances. We went out of the clothing business in 1964. Granddaddy paid me five cents on the dollar, so I'd save up and then go across the street to the drugstore with about three dollars and buy a cheeseburger, French fries and a milkshake with a dollar left over.*

B.W. Moncrief General Merchandise. *Courtesy of Marc Parker.*

My granddaddy put color televisions on New Year's Day in the front window so people could watch the Bowl games in color. That was the 1960s. People were very weird about buying microwaves back then, thinking they'd get radiation in their stomachs. Mayor Bill Gillespie's daddy bought the first microwave from the store and wanted me to bring it to his house after hours so he could cook something in it for us. We decided on steak, and I told him I liked mine where a little blood falls out. Well, he put the steaks in the microwave and didn't pay too much attention to them while he was pouring us a drink. After about thirty-five minutes, the bottle of whiskey was gone, he looked at the steaks, and they were as tough as they could be.

> *Granddaddy gave out Juicy Fruit chewing gum at the store for years. That was his trademark. I never will forget the IRS auditor coming and looking at the ledgers (there were no computers). He looked at the books, and asked, "You spent $150 on chewing gum?" We had just gotten our order in, took them down there and showed them all of those packs of Juicy Fruit. After Granddaddy died, the headlines in the* Prattville Progress *said, "Hollie Moncrief dies: A smile, a joke and a stick of Juicy Fruit chewing gum." It was a tradition that continued for fifty years.*

A Brief History of the Fountain City

Jamie Hatfield Moncrief stated:

A man came to my office one day when I was working for the mayor, and he said, "I don't know whether this will mean anything to you or not, but when I was cleaning out my barn the other day, I remembered Mr. Moncrief asking me to hold on to the original light post that was at the store, that it might be worth something one day." I told him that I was sure the City of Prattville could find a place for the light post. Today, it's located at the front of the garden on Main (where the building burned down). That light was one of the original power company lights.

The following is an ad for Moncrief's store displayed in the *Prattville Progress* on January 1, 1948:

Moncrief's, Autauga's Most Complete Department Store: Hollie Moncrief, Whit Moncrief—"As we enter the New Year, we reaffirm our policy of constantly trying to serve our customers better, of bringing to you the fullest measure of mercantile service. This year—as in the past—we pledge our renewed efforts to please you in 1948."

Before running for Autauga County circuit clerk, Whit Moncrief served as the county coroner for ten years because he really wanted to help people. He wanted to make a difference in the world, but the job did not come without heartache, as Whit realized when responding to an emergency call one night:

On March 8, 1991, I got a call on a Friday night that there had been a wreck on Highway 82. There were three white pickups at the scene. It was obvious that there were deaths. I recognized a truck. I looked up at Captain Oates and said, "Damn. I'm sorry, but that's my brother." She immediately started calling for help. I just screamed and screamed. Denise [Oates] said that I let out a blood-curdling scream. We determined later that a drunk driver had killed him. I had just left my birthday party. My brother was a father with two young children. It changed my life. Daddy had died five months earlier, and Daddy's sister died the previous year.

According to the *Gadsden Times* of March 13, 1991:

Autauga County Coroner Whit Moncrief said it was a "mind-boggling feeling" to investigate a wreck which killed his brother, but he didn't ask to be relieved of the duty. Moncrief was at a party to celebrate his 37th birthday Friday night when he received a call that a fatal accident had occurred on US 82 near Prattville. When he arrived to identify the wreck's two victims, he learned that one was his brother, thirty-three-year-old Samuel Moncrief of Booth. The three-car wreck killed a man in another vehicle, Harold Ray Crow, forty-seven, of Prattville, and injured a twenty-year-old Prattville woman who was in the third vehicle.

Rex Musgrove

There is definitely much debate over where the first drugstore was in America. Some claim it was established in New Orleans around 1823. Supposedly, the first registered pharmacist started the drugstore. But most scholars agree that the real American drugstore began around the time of the Civil War because many more drugs were discovered after 1860 and medical knowledge was more prevalent than before this time.

Rex Musgrove's family business began as Prattville Drug Company and became a Rexall in 1913. Rexall was the brainchild of Louis Kroh Liggett, a Detroit patent medicine salesman who created a manufacturing cooperative for franchised drugstores at the turn of the twentieth century. In 1902, Liggett and thirty-nine other druggists launched a new company chartered as United Drug Company, and "Rexall," signifying "King of all," was registered as the primary trademark. The first orders of Rexall proprietary medicines were shipped in mid-March 1903.

According to Musgrove:

> *They were franchised stores, but all you agreed to do was to carry and promote the Rexall products. They made a comparable product to every product sold. They went all the way up to the 1970s, and then they sold to Kraft, and everything got changed around. When my mother got pregnant, they told my daddy if it were a boy, he would have to name him Rex for Rexall. So, that's all I've ever been known as, all my life, is Rex Musgrove.*
>
> *Drugstores from the late 1800s all the way up to the 1970s and '80s were gathering places for people. Our drugstore had the first radio in town, and everybody came to listen to the radio. We had an old Victrola, which I still have. Drugstores had soda fountains and tobacco departments because*

Prattville Drug Co. soda fountain. *Courtesy of Rex Musgrove.*

they had to make a living. There weren't enough drugs in those days to be sold to make a living. You just had five or six different drugs, and people hardly ever needed them. You made your money off the soda fountain and anything else you sold. But they were gathering places, and if people were expecting news, the drugstore was left open.

Regular hours were anywhere from six or seven in the morning until around ten o'clock at night or until the last customer was gone. We had Sunday hours, so we opened from nine to eleven, closed for church and opened back up from three until six. We did that for years until everybody knew me. Then, if they needed something when we weren't open on Sunday, they'd just call me at home, and I would go back to the store and get it for them.

My father used the apothecary grinder to crush pills. When I began work there in the 1960s, all of that was being phased out, and everything went from the grinding and powders to the compressed tablets. My dad remembers grinding and making powders. You'd have to weigh out the powder, put it in a little cellophane envelope, fix twenty or thirty of them in a little box and then the customer would take our powder out, put it in water and drink it. That was when you were mixing medicine. You had more syrups than today because the first truly mode of medication was powder and liquids.

You didn't have compressed tablets. Then, the next thing was a capsule, so you made your powder and had to fill the capsules. One of the last things we were compounding was a suppository. We knew how to do it.

Dr. Smith opened Prattville Drug Co. in 1907, and my uncle, Maury McWilliams, came to work for him as a young pharmacist right out of Auburn. Maury went into the service, came back to the store in 1920 and worked with Dr. Smith. The drugstore, however, burned in 1928. Everything was lost, but he rebuilt it right there on the same location. Then, Dr. Smith died, and Maury bought the building and the business from his widow, and it stayed in our family—Maury McWilliams; my father, Gordon Musgrove; and then myself in 1999 when I sold it to CVS. I didn't have anyone coming along after me that wanted the store.

My uncle and dad were very progressive, so if somebody came in the drugstore and asked for something they didn't have, they'd immediately put it in stock. The drugstore, over the years, handled Shakespeare rods and reels and a full line of paint because nobody else sold paint in town. It was Sherwin-Williams paint. In the 1920s, we got into jewelry and china. We carried fine diamonds, fine jewelry and Gorham silver and became a bridal registry and a drugstore all in one, so the name became Prattville Drug & Gifts.

They hired a delivery boy in the drugstore about 1930. His mom said, "He is twelve, but he is big for his age. He needs a job real bad." This was in the middle of the Depression, and the drugstore was just hanging on by a string, but my uncle hired him with pay being a meal or two every day and maybe a dollar or two a week. Buster Hall died at seventy-two years old and had worked for us sixty years as a delivery and cleanup man. He was always told to be courteous and nice to the customers, and everybody in town liked him. He was told, "When you go to somebody's house and see a newspaper in the yard, pick it up and take it to the door. If a widow needs a light bulb changed, do it for her." My dad and uncle noticed that in the month of December, Buster was making more money in tips than they were making on sales!

The following is an ad in the *Prattville Progress* that was displayed for Prattville Drug Company on January 1, 1947:

How long have you worn that old truss? Be correctly fitted with a new one today—feel better—look better—work better. Come in and talk with us—trusses—anklets—elastic stockings—knee braces—abdominal supporters and other types of supporters.

Musgrove home, built 1913. *Courtesy of Rex Musgrove.*

Rex Musgrove recalled:

> *A Western Union was there at the drugstore during the time of World War II. My daddy had a lady whose main job was to get to the Teletype machine and write down the messages that were coming in. The worst job my daddy ever had was to get the message a serviceman was killed. It was my dad's job to get the telegram to the family. The lady who was running the telegraph was at lunch one day when the telegraph bell went off. Daddy got the message, and the message was that her husband had been killed.*

Musgrove's family dates back to the days when Prattville founder Daniel Pratt began to plot out the city, and the McWilliams family came to Autauga County in the late 1840s. A.K. McWilliams built the home that is currently used by the Autauga County Heritage Association and the City of Prattville as Prattaugan Museum. This antebellum home is listed on the National Register of Historic Places as inclusive in the Daniel Pratt Historic District.

Gene Kerlin

Gene Kerlin came to Prattville at about eight years old, and now he has lived into his eighties. He volunteers a couple times a week at the Prattaugan Museum, greeting visitors with a big smile, eager to talk about the history of the city which he is so knowledgeable. Kerlin's wife, Nita, was the daughter of former Prattville mayor Williamson Allen Glover, who served the city in that position from 1952 until 1956 and also served on the city council for many years.

Kerlin's folks were cotton farmers in the beginning; his dad later became a carpenter and then went into the grocery business. In 1941, Kerlin's father ran a store called H.J. Kerlin & Son in downtown Prattville, located where the Pasta Pizzeria & Grill is now. Harvey James Kerlin Sr. served on the city council (with only two other men) for the town of Prattmont in the late 1940s. Prattmont was a small community between Prattville and Montgomery. In later years, it was annexed into the city limits of Prattville.

Gene Kerlin recalled:

> *Prattmont was a sixteen- or eighteen-block area (the town itself) and was a subdivision developed in 1920. It extended down to where the McDonald's is now, all the way to Lumber Junction. Skyline Shopping Center was on the edge of it. The town of Prattmont consisted of seven service stations, a pottery place, two cafés and a couple businesses. There was no industry, so there was no way to sustain a city. There was a song about Prattmont. It went something like: "Beautiful Prattmont town where Highway 82 intersects 31 in beautiful Prattmont town." Prattville brought Prattmont in about 1953. The Pratt-Mont Drive-In was one of the oldest drive-ins in the state. It was located out in the cotton fields.*

The following are ads in the *Prattville Progress* that were displayed in 1947–48 for Prattmont:

> *Now specializing in pit barbecue steaks and chicken dinners—Shirley and Christy Soter, Operators*

> *Try Byrd's old-fashioned barbecue sandwiches—Byrd's Place, Prattmont.*

Prattmont. *Courtesy of Alfred Wadsworth.*

Skyline Shopping Center. *Courtesy of Rex Musgrove.*

Blue Moon Café. *Courtesy of Rex Musgrove.*

The Coburn family opened the Pratt-Mont Drive-In Theater in 1949. In those days, drive-ins were used primarily as a place to meet friends and see a movie without dressing up or spending too much money. People would bring their coolers and lawn chairs and just do their own thing, eating or playing pinball at the snack bar, not really caring too much about what was playing on the screen. They just wanted to socialize. The Coburns built a playground so that children could run about while the adults were talking. The Pratt-Mont charged five dollars a carload, and children under twelve got in free. The drive-in closed in 1986. After closing, the area was used for flea markets until the entire property was demolished in 1990 to make way for an expansion of Highway 82.

Kerlin calls the City Café, the Prattville Drug Company soda fountain and the Lyric Theater some of his favorite downtown hot spots. The following is an ad listing the movies at Lyric Theater in the first part of January 1948:

It Happened on Fifth Avenue; *On Saturday—Roy Rogers and his horse Trigger in* On the Old Spanish Trail, Jesse James Rides Again; *Saturday Night Owl Show 10:45 PM—*It's a Joke, Son; *Sunday &*

Monday—Mother Wore Tights*; Tuesday & Wednesday*—Wife Wanted*; Our next action packed Tuesday & Wednesday serial will be* The Vigilantes.

Kerlin also noted:

> *Dr. Wilkinson's drugstore was right next to the Prattville Drug Company. His office was in the back of the store. Ward Drugstore was located on the lot next to Paravicini's. They made medicines from herbs. There was a full-blooded Indian that lived in the county that would come and bring herbs to Dr. Ward. The Indian sat out front on Saturdays with a chair, and he'd pull your teeth with his hands. People would say, "He can't pull my wisdom tooth with his hands!" But, he did. They also said that he would pull perfectly good teeth on a bet!*

Mac Gipson

Hannibal McNeal Gipson Jr. (Mac Gipson), a lifelong Autauga County resident, is retired from Gipson's Auto Tire, Inc., in Prattville and Millbrook as owner and president and is a former member of the Alabama House of Representatives, representing Autauga and Elmore Counties. He is currently administrator of the Alabama Alcoholic Beverage Control Board. Gipson and his wife, Mary Lee, have four children:

> *Mary Lee and I met on a blind date. We were introduced by a girl whose grandfather lived on Bridge Creek. There was a big party at the clubhouse there, and we laughed at the adults who were half drunk. You could hear them on the lake. Daddy was a steward in the Methodist church, which back then was like a deacon. He signed a petition and saw a need to tax alcohol even though it was prohibitive in the Methodist discipline. They kicked him out of the church because he signed the petition.*
>
> *Where the city hall is today was a two-story building. Upstairs was one great big room where the scouts met. I was in Troop 225. On weekends, it was called Teen Tavern. Teen Tavern consisted of a jukebox, a bare floor and a counter. That was the teenage hangout. Of course, there was no alcohol. There was a Chrysler dealership next door, and next to it was the*

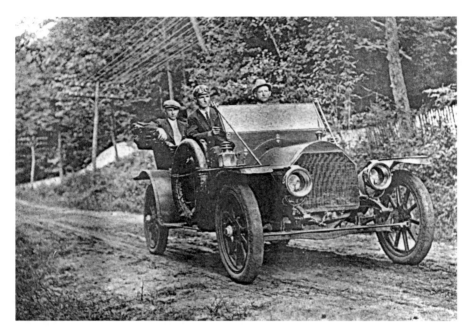

Early resident driving a Cadillac. *Courtesy of Rex Musgrove.*

Lyric Theater. The projector was a carbide lamp projector. Invariably, the film would hang and catch on fire. The siren was on top of the building, and it would go off because they had to summon the volunteer fire department. You'd mill around outside while they'd get the fire under control and then go back in and finish watching the movie.

Sam Abney

Sam Abney recalled:

When I was a kid, we'd swim in the creek. Back in those days, the cotton mill dumped their dye into the creek. You might go in swimming, and the water would be blue, but before you could come out, it would have turned red. The dye would wash right off. My daddy worked at the pool during summers. The pool was filled with water from an artesian well, and boy, was it cold!

Shady Lane Farm has been the Abney home for five generations. Sam and his wife, Mary Lou, a retired elementary school teacher, currently live in the original house, which has been moved to its present location not too far from where it was built. Abney and his wife raise Boer goats on their forty-acre farm within the city limits of Prattville. Their family of goats has been in Christmas nativities, parades, shows, educational displays and civic functions.

In March 1867, Captain Zachariah Abney, Sam's great-grandfather, established himself in Prattville where he practiced law and took up farming. He served Autauga County as register in Chancery from 1883 until his death and was married to Alexandria Victoria Doster. Their son, Zachariah Abney Jr., and Marion Frances Bowen are Sam's grandparents:

> *My great grandpa never had a Confederate grave marker, so the family got him one, and they had it over at my dad's house. My dad was dying of cancer at the time. One of his friends came over and saw that marker with the name "Zach Abney" on it. Zach was my dad's name also, so the friend started crying and said, "Y'all got his grave marker all ready before he died!" My grandmother's sister, Alice, would come to visit us. Alice's husband, Charlie Reynolds, was a farmer. During the Depression, pecan trees were a real commodity. Charlie noticed some of his trees were missing. He found them and called the sheriff. He said, "Let's go. I know who stole my trees." The sheriff asked, "How are you going to prove those are your pecan trees?" Charlie said, "Dig one up." On the root of that pecan tree, he had a piece of metal that said, "C.D. Reynolds."*

Shopping

Gene Kerlin recalled:

> *The grand opening of Grant Plaza shopping center was held in October 1972. The city had Blue Laws back then that would restrict the time a store was open on Sunday. Well, Grant's broke the law. The manager was Jewish, and he didn't observe Christmas. All the churches were in an uproar because this store was open all day on Sunday. In the little town of Prattville, everything closed on Sunday, and even the drugstores would only open for three hours. Grant's was open from nine to ten, and ten o'clock was pretty late back then.*

Grant Plaza Grand Opening. *Courtesy of Alfred Wadsworth.*

W.T. Grant's was a chain of variety stores that went bankrupt in 1976. Other shopping centers in Prattville include Pratt Plaza, which is usually the site of the beginning of parades, and Midtown Shopping Center, which was redeveloped in 2000 to entail the renovation of a 100,000-square-foot retail center with Winn Dixie Marketplace. For those old enough to remember, the Big Bear grocery store was located at the Prattville Square Shopping Center, and that area underwent a transformation a few years ago to include remodeling of Comala Credit Union. Premiere Place is composed of 354,000 square feet of retail, including the Walmart Super Center anchor that opened in August 1996. Crestview Shopping Center contained IGA Food Liner and the Cotton Shop in the 1960s.

Rex Musgrove remembered, "We opened a branch of the drugstore in the Crestview Shopping Center. It was Crestview Rexall Drugs. The shopping center was renamed Heritage Place."

High Point Town Center includes approximately 900,000 square feet of retail space with Bass Pro Shops, J.C. Penney, Belk, Best Buy and

Parade downtown. *Courtesy of Rex Musgrove.*

Prattville Square. *Courtesy of Rex Musgrove.*

High Point Town Center. *Courtesy of Marc Parker.*

Publix. The complex, plagued with occupancy problems almost from the beginning, primarily caused by an economic downturn, was sold at an auction in July 2011 due to mortgage foreclosure. Mayor Bill Gillespie stated that this sale would not have an adverse effect on Prattville's economy. It is yet to be determined if the development fills to capacity with retail; however, the shopping area across the road entertains a diverse offering of retailers and restaurants primarily due to the Sanford family of Prattville.

James (Jimmy) Sanford is the chairman of the board of Home Place Farms, Inc., and is a fourth-generation cotton producer whose great-grandparents began operations of a cotton farm in 1881. Part of the family's land, or about 750 acres of it, has been developed, and the retail area is called The Exchange, where Target, Kohl's, Academy Sports and Hobby Lobby are located. There are approximately ten outparcels left for sale, lease and future development, and it is hoped that some small shops within a twenty-two-thousand-square-foot area will be developed directly in front of Kohl's.

Catherine Porter, Jimmy Sanford's daughter and Home Place developer, noted:

> *It was a little sad to see my family's land become retail, but at the same time, Prattville has grown, and this east side of town has developed and grown. It's kind of neat to be able to use it for another purpose besides farming. It serves so many people, not only in Prattville, but also in the whole River Region. You're just hoping to provide something for somebody else and that you have an impact on their lives.*

7

MAJOR EVENTS AND OCCURRENCES

Floods

Floodplains in Prattville exist along both Autauga Creek and Pine Creek, two of the major creeks that flow through the city. The floodplain along Autauga Creek is quite expansive and encompasses most of the downtown area. Of course, when Daniel Pratt settled the area, the main thing he was looking for was a good source of water. Hence, as Pratt's industry was developed on the banks of Autauga Creek, he plotted the rest of the town nearby and, unfortunately, in the floodplain. The floodplain surrounding Pine Creek encompasses very little developed land because of its narrowness, but it does stretch from the southern corporate boundary to the northern boundary. When torrential rains came to the city in 1919, 1938 and 1939, Main Street flooded, usually with waist-high water from the creek.

Rachel Deaile wrote in the *Montgomery Advertiser*:

> *In 1919, they took down the covered bridge to widen the creek and prevent further flooding. It wasn't until after the '38 and '39 floods that a government flood control project was being considered. Today, such a project would be a multi-million dollar venture. Barely coning out of the Great Depression and with the onset of WWII, money was scarce, and the flood control project was put on hold.*

Waist-high flood. *Courtesy of Rex Musgrove.*

The 1939 flood. *Courtesy of Rex Musgrove.*

A Brief History of the Fountain City

Prattville suffered extensive damage in August 1939 when the downtown business district was under six feet of water. The people formed a flood control committee and elected M.A. McWilliams as chairman. The Prattville Lions Club even sponsored an erosion control project.

Rex Musgrove recalled:

> My great uncle, Maury McWilliams, was out in a boat in downtown Prattville during the floods. The creek that you see today did not have the depth to it that it does now. You could walk to the end of the street and just wade out into the creek at one time. Once we had the floods, the Public Works Administration (PWA) came along, and the first project they had was to get in the creek and dredge it to give it depth so that the water would rise and fall within the banks of the creek. The creek has never risen and flooded again since that time, but we did have a couple of floods in the 1960s, and then one just a few years ago where it was a flash flood. They've solved the problem now where the water won't flood Main Street.
>
> McWilliams Branch (named after my family) is the creek that feeds the area. They just basically built the city over that Branch. It comes under Main Street and straight out in the creek. The problem is when you have about twelve inches of rain in an hour's time on Third Street, and when it comes under the street, the water gets damned up because of debris.

According to Gene Kerlin, "Red Devil Lake burst in the flood of August 1939. That was the worst flood Prattville ever had. The Red Devil Lake dam broke. A railroad trestle downtown was also destroyed in the flood."

On August 18, 1939, the *Biloxi Daily Herald* reported:

> The Alabama River was expected to crest at about fifty-two feet tonight. At Prattville, the ordinarily placid Autauga Creek suddenly became a raging torrent that caused an estimated $250,000 damage, and residents and merchants began the task of cleaning up. Officials believed the creek would near its normal flow by midnight.

The *Sarasota Herald-Tribune* of August 16, 1939, read:

> Autauga Creek sprung into a raging torrent by an all-night downpour, which poured through this central Alabama town today, flooding streets, stores and homes. No loss of life was reported, but City Clerk A.E. McCrary said

Left: Flood, circa 1930s. *Courtesy of Rex Musgrove.*

Below: Flood on Main. *Courtesy of Rex Musgrove.*

Downtown flood, circa 1930s. *Courtesy of Rex Musgrove.*

all but one of a dozen to fifteen families at nearby Allenville had been evacuated. An estimated dozen families had been forced to abandon their homes. McCrary estimated the creek had risen thirteen feet and that half the town's stores were flooded or threatened. Sandbags which merchants began throwing up around midnight were protecting many places.

The last major flood in the city where water actually stood several feet on Main Street occurred in 1939. Stated in the Flood Control Act of 1941 (authorizing the construction of certain public works on rivers and harbors for flood control and for other purposes): "The project for local flood protection at Prattville, Alabama, on Autauga Creek, a tributary of the Alabama-Coosa River, is hereby authorized to be constructed substantially in accordance with the recommendation of the Chief of Engineers at an estimated cost of $530,000."

On September 1, 2000, eight inches or more of rain fell in the city within a few hours. Storm drains and sanitary sewers overflowed, damaging many businesses and residences, but fortunately flooding was kept to a minimum. In May 2009, some homes and downtown businesses suffered only minor water damage when almost five inches fell in a matter of two hours.

Civil Rights and Stokely Carmichael

It might be necessary to talk a little about the atmosphere in the South, and in Prattville, Alabama, during the turbulent 1960s before the 1967 incident with Stokely Carmichael is discussed. Life in the pre–civil rights South basically denied its black citizens many of the most basic human rights. There was a white drinking fountain and a "colored" drinking fountain. In those days, black people were referred to either as "colored" or "Negro," with the term "African American" used decades later.

Schools were segregated under the constitutional doctrine of "separate but equal," which allowed states to educate white and black children in separate, purportedly equal facilities.

Retired Prattville schoolteacher Nelda Cain recalled:

> *We didn't exist. They saw us, but they didn't see us. We were not people. Black people didn't truly exist. It's as if God didn't create us. We were just something that was in the way. If I rubbed my hand on you, you wouldn't turn black, so what was the difference? We're all human beings. It hurt, but there was nothing you could do.*

The "separate but equal" doctrine was eventually overturned in 1954, but there were still poorer services for blacks and restrictions on voting rights limiting them throughout the United States. The next few years saw Martin Luther King Jr. leading the famed Montgomery Bus Boycott and, in 1957, serving as the first president of the Southern Christian Leadership Conference (SCLC), an organization founded to coordinate and support nonviolent direct action to desegregate bus systems around the South. It eventually expanded the focus beyond buses to ending all forms of segregation. King delivered his "I Have a Dream" speech during the 1963 March on Washington and the next year received a Nobel Peace Prize for his work to end racial segregation and racial discrimination through nonviolent means.

In Prattville, Alabama, the "Magnificent Seven" was formed in the 1950s to start a voter registration drive. The group consisted of Willie Lee Wood, Sr., Tony Davis, Lafayette Alexander, Frank Gipson Sr., Ivory Hoyt, Howard Lamar and Warren Lamar. Howard and Warren were cousins. At that time, there were only about seven registered black voters in Autauga County. The "Magnificent Seven" had to meet in private because the Ku Klux Klan was active in the area.

A Brief History of the Fountain City

Delois Sager, daughter of Willie Lee Wood Sr., recalled:

The KKK shot into our house. Our baby sister was in the bed. She wasn't hurt and was so young that she didn't know what was going on. Daddy stood over a cross burning in our yard holding a shotgun. I stood by Daddy. We didn't have any protection because all of the law enforcement officers were KKK members. Daddy said that the only way for change to happen is to vote those people out and always told us that if you knew in your heart that you were right, do not be afraid to speak up or stand up. He said, "Before I stop, they will have to kill me because I won't stop. I'm going to fight until I can get every black person in Autauga County registered to be voters."

Wood, born in Autauga County in 1921, married the former Elmira Davis, and the pair had seven children: six girls and one boy. He attended North Highland High School and Alabama State University. Wood was a member of the Alabama Democratic Conference of Alabama and Autauga County, the Autauga County Heritage Association and the Library Association in Prattville and was one of the founders of the Autauga County Improvement Association, whose goal it was to get blacks registered to vote.

Former city council president Mike Renegar remembered:

Current city council member Willie Wood's father was part of the Martin Luther King movement through this area. I think he was very closely connected to Dr. King. I can remember separate restrooms and water fountains here. They integrated during my junior year of high school. Fortunately, we meshed together without many problems at school. It is sad we had to go through discrimination.

Wood ran for city council several times and lost each time, but he was the first black to run for office in Autauga County. His only son, Willie Lee Wood Jr., succeeded in that endeavor and became, in 1988, the first black elected to the council, recently winning his seventh term in office.

Delois Sager said:

Daddy ran for coroner and city council, but nobody was going to allow him to get in office. Daddy was still fighting as he became older and wanted to see a black person on the council. He talked Brother [Willie Lee Wood Jr.] into running. Brother was real young and afraid, and he

*didn't know anything about politics. Daddy and Brother were real close.
I guess because Brother had such good character, he won, and I think
Daddy won, too, that day.*

About a decade after "The Magnificent Seven" was organized, on the
night of February 14, 1967, a forty-three-year-old black man, Charles
Rasberry, became involved in his neighbor's gun battle with three white
men. That neighbor, James Huffman, also a black man, was arrested for
the murder of a white car salesman, and Rasberry was also arrested on
a murder charge in connection with the incident. A couple days later,
Rasberry was dead. Two stories circulated about his death. A state NAACP
field director claimed that Rasberry said to him that he was shot in the back
after police told him he could go free. The other story was that Rasberry
was shot after he twice struck a police officer in an escape attempt as he
was being taken to jail. James Huffman was found innocent at his trial by
an all-white jury.

According to Prattville resident Dan Houser of the Autauga County
Improvement Association, a call went out to all black students to stay out
of school at least one day in protest of Rasberry's killing, but attendance at
Autauga County School was reported as normal. A few months later, Houser
would be involved in a day of reckoning in Prattville involving infamous
black activist Stokely Carmichael.

Nelda Cain recalled:

*I would see Dan every morning. He'd come and get my uncle because they
worked together in construction. He was abusive and drank a lot. The cops
beat him up in jail and kicked him out for dead. That was the same day as
the shootout when Stokely Carmichael was here.*

Attempts had been made by responsible groups, both white and black,
to work out their various grievances and misunderstandings, but these had
not been settled to the satisfaction of either side when Carmichael appeared
on the scene on June 11, 1967. On that hot summer afternoon, about one
hundred demonstrators gathered in the yard of the First Baptist Church,
across the street from the Autauga County Improvement Association in the
Happy Hollow neighborhood, for a scheduled meeting. The speaker was
Student Nonviolent Coordinating Committee (SNCC) chairman and activist
Carmichael, who brought the phrase "Black Power" into the spotlight and
turned it into a rallying cry for young blacks.

That afternoon and into the night, as Carmichael was speaking, rioting and violence was breaking out in several major U.S. cities. In Prattville, according to eyewitness reports, Carmichael's speech triggered a heated exchange with local police officer Kenneth "Kennedy" Hill, who months earlier had shot and killed Charles Rasberry. Black citizens had asked the mayor to fire Hill, and when that didn't happen, they asked Carmichael how to remove him from the force.

Carmichael told the crowd:

> *We advocate that all black people get some guns and learn how to use them.*
> *The only way to get Kennedy Hill off the force is to organize the black power*
> *in this area and use your guns. Black Power! Black Power! Black Power!*

Officer Kennedy Hill retorted, "Listen you. You don't go 'round shouting and going on, hear?"

"Would you like to speak to me? I'm Mr. Carmichael."

"I don't give a damn who you are! You've got no business shouting like that," Officer Hill replied.

The conversation between Carmichael and Hill escalated with more irate exchanges and ended with an arrest. Hill struck Carmichael after securing him in a police car, jerked a camera from the neck of a photographer for the *Southern Courier* and snatched a tape recorder from Norman Lumpkin, a radio news reporter. Gunshots fired from the vicinity of a police car scattered the crowd, and some forty people, including Houser, took cover inside his home.

In the words of Judge Frank M. Johnson Jr., following a four-day hearing that same year in October, "Until about 2:00 AM on Monday, June 12, Prattville, Alabama, literally became an armed camp." State troopers, Autauga County deputies, Prattville police officers and Alabama national guardsmen surrounded Houser's house, where Sheriff Phillip Wood used a loudspeaker to order everyone outside. Houser and almost a dozen others were arrested. All but Houser were taken to the Autauga County Jail. He was taken straight to the Prattville City Jail. Prior to his release late the next day, without being charged with any crime, Houser was severely beaten about the face, head and body either by police officers or by persons unknown.

Nelda Cain said:

> *I don't know when Dan turned militant. He ended up marrying a white*
> *woman after being married thirty years. He already had a beautiful family.*

HAPPY HOLLOW

Known as Fair Road, Sixth Street from Northington Street to the big curve was called "Happy Hollow". The road went to the Fair home place but also curved right, into Warren Circle. Here stood a small frame church where the congregation's enthusiastic preaching, singing, and shouting led to the name Happy Hollow Church. Bethleham Colored Methodist Episcopal was relocated in 1947 to Chestnut and Sixth, and renamed Bethlehem Christian Methodist Episcopal Church.

Within the Hollow the "Spring", one of Prattville's signature artesian wells, provided water for drinking, cooking, bathing and washing before the city had a central water system. The mail route ended at the home of Miss Molly Burt where all the neighbors picked up their mail. These gathering places made for a close-knit community.

A traditional African American neighborhood, the Hollow was home for domestic workers, farm laborers, landowners and sharecroppers. Descendants of these families became leaders in Prattville and beyond: educators, nurses, doctors, accountants, carpenters, armed forces and ministers.

Beloved as a place to grow up even in segregated times: black and white children could not go to school together but played together in the branch that runs the length of The Hollow.

ALABAMA HISTORICAL ASSOCIATION 2010

Happy Hollow marker. *Courtesy of Marc Parker.*

Many people almost lost their homes getting him out of jail, and then he turned around and married a white woman. [Governor] Lurleen Wallace sent the National Guard to his house that night. There are bullet holes here on the porch.

Houser and Sallie Hadnott, another local civil rights activist, asked district judge Frank M. Johnson Sr. in federal court to issue an order directing Prattville and Autauga County officers to give blacks equal treatment in the city. The police, on the other hand, wanted an order against disturbances or other illegal activity by civil rights groups. Houser accused the police of beating him, saying he suffered small fractures, a broken nose and eye injuries. Police chief O.C. Thompson and other officers said that no black people were mistreated.

A historical marker stands today in the Happy Hollow neighborhood where the incident took place. Part of it reads:

A traditional African American neighborhood, the Hollow was home for domestic workers, farm laborers, landowners and sharecroppers. Descendants of these families became leaders in Prattville and beyond: educators, nurses, doctors, accountants, carpenters, armed forces and ministers. Beloved as a place to grow up even in segregated time; black and white children could not go to school together but played together in the branch that runs the length of the Hollow.

Shannon Paulk

On August 16, 2001, less than a month before the September 11 attacks on America, eleven-year-old Shannon Paulk was abducted from the Candle Stick Park neighborhood in Prattville. The last time this young girl was seen alive, she was talking to an unknown man in his late thirties to mid-forties at about 2:30 p.m. that day. A couple of her friends approached them, but since Paulk never introduced the man, it was felt she did not know him. To the happy, trusting child, everyone in the trailer park community was considered a friend and not a stranger.

Former Prattville mayor Jim Byard Jr., who was the city's highest-ranking officer at the time of Paulk's disappearance, recalled, "That was a horrible time. Prattville grew up in the days and weeks after Shannon went missing. We had our eyes opened to the evil in the world, and we didn't like what we saw."

When Paulk disappeared, a nationwide search began, and local and federal police and neighbors formed a task force. Their tireless efforts came to an unspeakable end two months later when hunters found the child's body in the woods of Autauga County. Prattville enjoyed a quiet, back-to-the-land lifestyle in 2001, with a population of only about twenty-four thousand, and had long prided itself on its low crime rate. This heinous atrocity shook the tightknit community to the core.

Former Prattville police chief Alfred Wadsworth said:

> *The Shannon Paulk case is the one I think about all of the time. It was real hot that August when she disappeared. We had more people who wanted to help search than we could actually control, but that was a good problem. The investigation is ongoing, and hopefully sometime in the future, there will be some type of conclusion. Cases involving children bother me more than anything else.*

A description of the man Paulk met that day was given to police by her two friends. The case has been featured almost a dozen times on *America's Most Wanted*, the national television show that solicits tips on unsolved crimes. The Prattville City Council authorized a $10,000 reward for any information leading to an arrest and conviction. In 2007, actress Pauley Perrette, who plays Abby Sciuto on the television series *NCIS*, doubled the reward. She was raised in Alabama and all over the southern United States. Despite the best efforts of everyone involved, the Shannon Paulk murder remains the town's most infamous crime.

According to Prattville police chief Tim Huggins:

> *The case is still active, and we are still working, still chasing leads. The task force, made up of the Prattville police department, FBI, Alabama Bureau of Investigation and the Autauga County Sheriff's Office, is still in place.*

The Fire That Lit Up the Sky

Remember Gardner Hale's comment about a factory not going up in smoke as long as Daniel Pratt had stock in it? Well, the following story describes the irony of that statement made over 150 years ago. Of course, Daniel Pratt has long since passed away, but the three-story, block-long Gurney Manufacturing building, a structure he erected in the 1850s, was destroyed by fire on a warm September night in 2002.

Former Prattville police chief Stanley Gann recalled:

> *The gurney building was the biggest fire on my watch. Several juveniles in the basement were playing, started a fire and left it unattended. There were oil-soaked floors in the building. That kept the dust down, but it made the fire worse. We probably got the fire under control in four to six hours, but we were there twenty-four to thirty-six hours just monitoring because we saved the little white building on this end, and on the other end where that main old building connected those warehouses—we stopped it there.*

The fire was jointly investigated by local and state law enforcement officers, and a few months later, five teenagers were sentenced to juvenile corrections facilities for setting the fire that destroyed the Prattville landmark. According to a newspaper article, the teen who admitted to starting the fire was sentenced to Department of Youth Services custody, and the other four went to boot camp.

The Gurney was part of the old Pratt millworks that manufactured cotton gins since before the Civil War. Fortunately, the skilled, courageous firefighters saved the rest of the historic factory and the nearby downtown buildings. In his own words, this is the story of the fire from one of those brave heroes, twenty-six-year Prattville firefighter Guy Boutin:

> *I was home in bed in the wee hours of September 10, 2002, when a phone call jarred me out of a routine sleep. On a cell phone at the other end was my good friend and current circuit clerk, Whit Moncrief, speaking to me in a hurried, urgent voice, "Guy! Get down here! It's on fire! It's gonna go down! Gurney! It's burning down!" I knew Whit's report was accurate because he always monitored fire department traffic and from his home on Upper Kingston would have no problem beating PFD units to the scene responding from Station One.*

Mill Lake fire. *Courtesy of Tommy Brown.*

I tossed the covers back and jumped from bed, not bothering to click the light on. My wife asked in a concerned tone, "What is it?" "It's Gurney. It's on fire big time," I answered. A silence followed before her next words, "Please be careful." I said to her, "You know, I will be okay. I don't know when I will be home. If you don't hear anything from me, don't worry because this is gonna take awhile."

The Gurney Mill was the one building every firefighter talked about. From the time Prattville had a fire department, personnel discussed what to do when the "big one" came in and what it would feel like to roll into downtown on a first unit with a working fire in the mill. Now, that night had come, and we were about to find out how many of us were true to his words.

I was winding down my career in the fire department that year. I'd spent most of my time assigned to Station Two, located on Fourth and Court Streets, just across the street from the mill and down a few blocks. It was literally a four-minute walk from my station office to the personnel building. I had been on countless pre-fire plans of the structure and had contributed significantly to the current plan on file.

A Brief History of the Fountain City

Over the years, I had responded to numerous EMS calls and small fires in the building that had been contained by the sprinklers. The building would have burned down if not for the system. I knew that for a fact, so when a few years earlier, Chief McGough stopped in Station Two to inform us the sprinkler system in the now-abandoned mill was going offline, to say I was aghast would be putting it lightly. "You know it's going to burn down, Chief," I said. "Yeah, but we don't know when. Review the pre-fire plans and see if there is anything we missed or could do better, and get back to me," the chief said.

I finished that review and passed it up the chain of command. Most changes related to the reality the building was now empty, unguarded and without sprinklers, and all were prime ingredients for mayhem or arsonists. If my timeline is correct, the one-hundred-year-old-plus building lasted five or six years without the sprinklers.

From my house to Station Two is a one-minute drive in a hurry (which I was), and as I crested the hill at Sixth and Woodvale, the entire western sky of Autauga County was orange. It was so bright I could have read a newspaper in my driveway. I knew this could be a dangerous and risky fire if we wavered even a little from our training. I was two years from retiring, but that thought didn't enter my mind as I focused on the task ahead.

The situation was grim, and if things were as bad as they looked, we would not be able to save the building. What we could do would be to keep it from getting any worse by allowing it to spread to any other businesses or homes in the area, and we had to do that without letting anyone get hurt.

And, I looked at it like this—if it was going to burn down, I wanted to be there.

I pulled into an empty Station Two, gathered my equipment and scampered down the street to the command post located in the now parking lot of the Pasta Mill at Third and Court Streets. First-in units were stretching lines and setting up. Whit's phone call put me on the scene within minutes of the original 911 call and way ahead of the official recall.

Court Street seemed ablaze. Fire was showing from every window on all floors. The heat was intense, and I could feel it on my face as I shot up the street to find the command post. The sounds of screaming men, radio traffic, fire trucks and spewing water cannons filled the night. It was the noise of a desperate situation because this fire had the real potential of spreading.

My assignment was to advance a hose line into the personnel building (separate from the mill) and prevent the fire from taking it. "Just get as many guys as you think you'll need and let me know when y'all are in operation," Chief McGough advised, as he turned to instruct another officer reporting to the command post.

I quickly grabbed four guys and said, "Put that down and come with me. We gotta get a hose line into that building or we're gonna lose it. From there, it can jump to the shops along Main Street, and if that happens, we're in a real mess," I said to them. I could see the white paint on the office starting to blister as the radiant heat coming from the mill worked it over.

It was a long hose lay from the fire truck to the fence gate that was padlocked with a chain, but we were ready for just that situation, broke out the bolt cutters to gain entry, then forced the office door open and entered the building. It was a long, dark crawl to the north door and windows that I knew to be there. From that vantage point, I could direct a fire stream on the fire building, not to suppress the fire, but to put in place a water curtain to block the radiant heat coming off the fire.

We found the door, and I yelled out to my crew, "Look here! When I open this door, it's gonna be hot so open the hose line quickly and get behind it." I jerked the door open, and the blast of heat felt like I was next to the space shuttle. "NOW! NOW! OPEN THE NOZZLE!" and I dove out of the door behind the way, but not before I got a shot of radiant heat. Our first order of business was to cool the north wall of the office building with our three-hundred-gallon-a-minute hose line, after which we placed a water curtain between the two buildings, effectively keeping the fire from jumping to the office.

The action of my crew that night was just one of similar actions taking place all around. North of us, crews were working just as hard to save a few warehouses. From my second-floor window, I could see Montgomery and Millbrook fire units on the street below. Fire hoses weaved and curved all over Court Street so much it looked like a plate of spaghetti was spread out before me.

The coolness of the water flowing from our hose line made our position tenable, and now it just became a question of waiting out the fire. Short of dumping the area in the Alabama River, we could not pour enough water on the blaze to quench it, but we did know it would eventually run out of fuel, and in the end, it would be a draw. The fire got Gurney, but we kept it from spreading, and more importantly, no one was seriously injured.

By daybreak, we were able to leave our hose line, come out of the building and report to "rehab," the magical place where firefighters are transformed from tired and worn out to "good to go" again. In rehab, I

Gurney fire. *Courtesy of Tommy Brown.*

sipped a sports drink while dogging my fellow firefighters and listening to comments like, "Man, did you see the front wall collapse?" and "I was so close I felt the wind."

With my son away in college, my wife was home alone. I wanted to call her, and there were plenty of phones around. I had a choice of three in a nearby ambulance, or I could just ask any of the nearby spectators for a phone. I could see hundreds of them behind the tape. But to call from a strange number or from a fire department number from an ambulance phone would have startled her to the point of breakdown, so I skipped that option for my personal phone. The only problem was that my phone was in my car a few blocks away.

With the urgency of the situation in the past, I slipped under the tape and sauntered the two blocks to Station Two and retrieved my phone from the front seat of my car. As I listened to the ring tones on the other end, I could picture the Caller ID lighting up with "Guy," and my wife answering the phone. She picked up, asking, "Oh, thank God, are you okay?"

"Yes, tired, but all good. We'll be here the rest of the day. I have no idea when I will be home. The cleanup will take days. Have you not turned on the TV?" "No. It would make it worse because if I didn't see you, I would worry," she answered. "OK. Well, get ready for work. From here, it's just another day," I said to her. We shared a few other things, and then I returned to my duty.

The PFD remained on the scene in some capacity for a week or more. Where the great mill once poured out goods by the ton, a now four-block hole fifteen feet deep stood full of smoldering debris and rubble. My crew was the unit sent to the site to remove the last of our equipment and to turn the scene over to the private sector.

The loss of Gurney will never be replaced. I grew up in Prattville. It was always there. I vividly recall the scent of dyes and yarn that seemed to seep from the place on certain days. It was not an unpleasant odor. It was just distinct. Now, anytime I catch a whiff of something similar, it takes me back to training runs that took me past the mill or spring days cooking out on the grill at Station Two.

A fountain and small park can now be found at the empty lot on the banks of Autauga Creek that was once home to Gurney. It seems to be a popular place for picture taking, especially at prom time or wedding season. Many people in those photos have no idea how the area once looked, like how the structure used to cast long shadows on Court Street as the sun set in the west on hot summer afternoons or the sound of the lunch whistle when it blew, calling workers back to work.

That is long gone, so it will be up to us to pass on to a new generation of Prattvillians that our city has a rich and detailed past to blend with the chrome and glass of the east side.

The buildings that were destroyed by the fire had been unoccupied since 1997, when Gurney went out of business. At that time, some individuals interested in preserving the structures purchased them. The nearby buildings containing the historic Continental Gin Shop were unharmed by the conflagration of September 10, 2002.

Former Prattville mayor Jim Byard Jr. recalled:

The evening of September 10 was filled with so much emotion because there were many people there watching our history burn. You felt helpless because you couldn't do anything but watch. I lived in East Prattville then, was on my way to the fire and heard them say that they needed to cut the power grid for downtown, so I knew it was bad. When I got to Station One by Walgreens, you could see the glow, and there was a Montgomery fire truck sitting there, so I knew we had already called in reserves. It was very eerie that night.

Twister Touches Down

Devastation slammed Prattville on the afternoon of February 17, 2008, when an EF3 tornado a quarter of a mile wide, with winds of about 155 miles per hour, touched down and struck the city, causing significant damage to several businesses and over two hundred homes. Some of the hardest-hit neighborhoods were Highland Ridge, Silver Hills, Prattville East and Overlook Estates on the east side of the city. Heavy damage was found along Cobbs Ford Road, a major city thoroughfare. The following is an account of a family's traumatizing experience as told to a friend:

My daughter and her family were in a tornado yesterday. They are all fine. Their garage door blew off, and the garage ceiling fell on the cars so they can't get them out of the garage. Their big trampoline is wrapped around a tree in a neighbor's yard. They've been evacuated from their house. The power lines are all down, so they are not sure when they can get back in. They stayed with friends last night. The kids' school was damaged and has no power. I'm just so thankful they are all uninjured. Praise God. Her husband helped the neighborhood men in digging out an old man who was bedridden, and his roof blew off. My daughter and her family rode out the storm in the bathroom covered with blankets and pillows. She said lots of trees and electric poles are down. Her son is very afraid of thunder and lightning, and I'm sure this won't help him be less afraid of storms.

Emergency crews went door-to-door in neighborhoods to search for trapped victims. Glass and windows were blown out of a KFC restaurant, a Food World grocery store was damaged, the roof collapsed on a Palm Beach Tan business and the glass doors were shattered at Walmart, where shoppers had been herded to the center of the store just moments before. The storm hit the roof and yanked the light fixtures out of the ceiling as people screamed. Cars were tossed around like toys and smashed to the ground.

Tornado-damaged home. *Courtesy of Marc Parker.*

Former secretary to Jim Byard Jr., Jamie Hatfield Moncrief, remembered:

> *I lived in Highland Ridge, which was hit pretty hard by the tornado. I walked up the street and realized we had houses flattened on that Sunday afternoon. I radioed the mayor and said, "We've been hit hard in my neighborhood." He said, "You don't know the half of it. I need you to walk to the command post. You can't drive because the debris is too bad on the roads." Thank goodness I lived behind Walmart, and the command post was at the nearby fire station. I was in shock while walking to see our town so devastated.*

Power poles were bent to the ground, and transformers were thrown in the air. Utility poles were snapped in half, blocking streets. Thousands of homes and businesses lost power. Debris was literally everywhere. Injuries numbered in the twenties, but thankfully no one was killed. As darkness fell, Mayor Jim Byard Jr. imposed a curfew on the city to retain control and prevent looting. Shelters opened up in churches, and a mobile hospital unit was set up outside the Kmart store. Kmart itself was simply decimated and was closed for a year. Walmart was closed for ten days for repairs.

Soon after the storm passed, fire departments arrived from the nearby cities of Montgomery, Millbrook and Wetumpka, about one hundred Alabama state troopers came to assist and hundreds of police officers were called to direct traffic among major thoroughfares. Byard and his brother Jeff, a senior administrator with the Alabama Emergency Management Agency, worked together to coordinate the recovery effort:

> *The tornado was very emotional. Most of the disasters we've had we could prepare for. We knew days in advance we had a big hurricane coming, and we were ready for that, but we didn't know the tornado was coming, and we were extremely blessed there were no deaths. We had good support from our neighbors and citizens, and we had local and state EMA and Public Safety folks who were right there propping me up, giving me advice, so it made it fairly easy to make it through the disaster. Our response was pretty impressive, city staff wise. I'm not speaking of me. I'm speaking of what our people did and what our citizens did as a whole.*

This tornado was one of at least nine that ripped across or touched down in the state on that day, also affecting Chilton, Coosa, Covington, Dallas and Lowndes Counties, as well as Autauga and Elmore, and it was one of the most significant outbreaks in central Alabama over the last several years.

"April's Fury," aptly named for one of the deadliest and most devastating tornado outbreaks in history, struck three years later. By the end of the day on April 27, 2011, more than sixty tornadoes had struck Alabama, killing more than 240 people, injuring thousands and destroying tens of thousands of homes. In total, 358 tornadoes were confirmed, and about 348 people were killed as a result of the four-day (April 25–28, 2011) outbreak, which affected many states throughout the southern and eastern United States.

8

SPORTING HIGHLIGHTS

The Lions' Den

The Prattville High School Lions football team has won five Alabama High School Athletic Association's Super 6 Class 6A state football titles (1984, 2006, 2007, 2008 and 2011). Since this is the only high school in town and football reigns supreme in Prattville and in the South, nary an empty parking space can be found during the fall season on game night at Stanley Jensen Stadium. The fans have been so ecstatic after a state championship win that they've adorned all of the trees downtown in toilet paper—with the mayor's permission, of course.

For two of those championship wins (2008 and 2011), the head coach who led the players to victories was Jamey DuBose. His coaching record at Prattville High School (PHS) is 45-11. DuBose was assistant coach for the title wins in 2006 and 2007. His legacy lasted eight years at the school until he resigned in early 2012, accepting a coaching job at a north Alabama school.

DuBose stated, "There is a great opportunity to play football in Prattville. That's why we try to encourage all our kids to play and be active. Football teaches hard work and discipline, and that's great for our youth, community and country that these kids are involved."

LPGA golfer Natalie Gulbis tossed the game coin in a 2009 game against Jefferson Davis, a Montgomery, Alabama high school, and the Prattville Lions easily took the victory by fifty-two points to zero. The Lions quarterback,

After a Lions championship. *Courtesy of Marc Parker.*

Sam Gibson, easily controlled the game and never looked back. He also led Prattville to the Alabama Class 6A state title in 2008 as the team's starting quarterback and was a three-star recruit to Louisiana State University (LSU).

Fans experienced a thrill-packed night during that same season when the Lions hosted Don Bosco Prep from New Jersey. It was a battle between two number-one teams, and ESPNU, a multimedia college sports brand, televised the matchup as part of the Old Spice High School Showcase. An estimated forty credentialed members of the ESPN crew were on site at Stanley Jensen Stadium to witness Don Bosco Prep's 35–24 victory. That was the second time Prattville has appeared on ESPNU; the first time was in 2008, when the Lions planted their paws firmly atop the Brentwood Academy Eagles (from Nashville, Tennessee) in a rout of 26–0.

Jamie Newberg, of ESPN recruiting, said, "What makes Prattville special? Like many small towns around the nation, football is more than just a game. It is a city's pride and joy."

Prattville native and PHS alumnus Chad Anderson was hired to enter the Lions' den and take over the reins at one of the state's most elite football programs when DuBose left PHS. This season, the Lions remain in Region Four, but pick up five schools near Birmingham on their 2012 schedule.

"It's like being handed the keys to a Porsche. Anderson's job is to keep it on the road and not crash it," said former Prattville football player and current New Orleans Saints safety Roman Harper.

Navistar LPGA Classic

The Robert Trent Jones Golf Trail features fifty-four holes of championship-caliber golf and is home to the Navistar Ladies Professional Golf Association (LPGA) Classic. The Trail was built by the people, one could say, because it was funded by the Retirement Systems of Alabama (RSA), whose members are retired teachers and state employees. When the Trail came to Prattville, David Whetstone was mayor, Jim Byard was president of the city council and Dean Argo was a council member. Argo recalled:

> Our economic developer at the chamber contacted me in 1996, and asked, "What do you think about us being the eighth stop on the Robert Trent Jones Golf Trail?" I was ecstatic because I knew what it would mean to this area and was shocked that it wasn't going to Montgomery. Anyway, she said that the RSA would come in and build the course, but the city would have to donate the land. She was talking to me to sort of get the feel of the Council. The RTJ Golf Trail got started in the early '90s, so it wasn't really an established thing in 1996, only four or five years old, but I told her I'd be glad to talk to the mayor.

Mayor David Whetstone was definitely a hard sell at first, but he and the city council members approved an expenditure of $6.5 million to buy the property on which the courses are located. After Whetstone's sudden death in office, Mayor Jim Byard continued to support the project, and in 1999, Prattville became home to the latest fifty-four holes of the Robert Trent Jones Golf Trail called Capitol Hill. It features three eighteen-hole championship courses: the Senator, the Legislator and the Judge.

Former mayor Jim Byard Jr. said:

Lorena Ochoa. *Courtesy of Marc Parker.*

It took a great deal of cooperation from both public and private entities to make this project a reality. We basically had an opportunity that a lot of other municipalities don't have. We funded the land for this project because we felt it would be an excellent economic development and tourism tool.

A dazzling collection of public golf courses in the state was the 1980s brainchild of Dr. David Bronner, CEO of the RSA. Enter legendary architect Robert Trent Jones Sr., the premier golf course architect in the world, and you have a match made in heaven. Once final approvals were given, the largest golf course construction project ever undertaken at one time anywhere in the world was underway with a collection of 468 holes of championship golf on eleven different sites across Alabama.

The *Wall Street Journal* said, "The Trail may be the biggest bargain in the country," and the *New York Times* called the Trail "some of the best public golf on earth." According to the readers of *Golf World*, the best public golf courses in the country are along Alabama's Robert Trent Jones Golf Trail. The top location is Grand National in Opelika, Alabama, the readers' favorite, with a score of 89.86, and the second top location is Capitol Hill in Prattville, with a score of 89.58.

The Navistar Classic, a women's professional golf tournament on the LPGA Tour, made its debut in September 2007 at the Capitol Hill location in Prattville. Maria Hjorth won the inaugural event, the now-retired top Mexican golfer Lorena Ochoa won consecutive titles in 2008 and 2009 and Katherine Hull won the next year and set the tournament scoring record.

Alexis "Lexi" Thompson became the youngest winner in the sixty-one-year history of the LPGA Tour by capturing a five-shot victory at the Navistar LPGA Classic in 2011, a mark broken in August 2012 by fifteen-year-old amateur Lydio Ko in the Canadian Women's Open. Thompson was sixteen years, seven months and eight days old at the time of the win.

In 2009, Thompson, at fourteen, became the youngest player in the field of 145 by qualifying for one of the two remaining spots in the Navistar LPGA Tournament in Prattville. Thompson told *Smashing Interviews Magazine* in an interview published on September 6, 2012, that her goal for the next four years is to work up to being on the first golf Olympics team.

In 2012, the event ran from September 17 to 23, with the tournament played the last four days. Stacy Lewis took the top honor by winning her third LPGA tour victory in five months and the second in Alabama, closing with a three-under sixty-nine to beat defending champion Lexi Thompson by two strokes. Her previous best at the Navistar in Prattville was a tie for sixth in 2011.

9

POLICE AND FIRE

Police Chief Alfred Wadsworth

Alfred Wadsworth's dad was chief deputy sheriff of Autauga County, and he was killed in the line of duty in 1952. Alfred and his twin brother, Albert, were five years old when that traumatic event happened, which made quite an impression on their young lives. They don't remember much about their father but do recall all the law enforcement officers in the home when he passed away. Not only did Alfred and Albert's dad influence his sons' career choices, but the brothers also spent much time at the fire department and around police officers when they were young.

Former police chief Alfred Wadsworth recalled:

> *I was a volunteer fireman and hung around Herman Scott and Donald McGough and played ball with chief deputy Hill, so I grew up around all those people. I started on the force July 20, 1970, and there were twelve or fourteen officers at that time. My brother (Albert) joined up a year after me. When I joined the department, the chief was O.C. Thompson. I became chief in 1993, and I always said that the mayor in office was the best one I ever served.*

In 1970, when Wadsworth became a brother in blue, the city's population was a little more than thirteen thousand. He recalls a safer time, not just for

Mayor Mac Gray and Alfred Wadsworth. *Courtesy of Alfred Wadsworth.*

Police officers, circa 1960. *Courtesy of Alfred Wadsworth.*

Prattville, but also for the rest of the country, when folks didn't even have to lock their front doors at night and one could just walk anywhere in town without being afraid. However, the crime rate is not at all terrible in the city now. In 2009, according to the Prattville Police Department's yearly report, 1,324 actual offenses were reported and 396 were cleared. There were eighty-three sworn police officers in that year, one cadet, five clerical workers, one dog warden and three civilian support officers for a total of ninety-three full-time employees.

Wadsworth said:

> *I think the people in the community make the difference. They become involved and care about the city as a whole. This is a church community. We have a prayer breakfast once a month with all the local ministers and elected officials. That type [of] fellowship is good, and it binds the community together.*

Effective on March 31, 2011, after forty years on the force, Wadsworth retired, taking advantage of retirement incentives offered in a budget package by Mayor Bill Gillespie. It was his wish that the retirement would help prevent further layoffs in the police department. His announcement came in the midst of the city changing mayors, losing its finance director and city clerk and also its fire chief. Tim Huggins, a twenty-six-plus veteran of the force, was selected to replace Wadsworth as chief of police.

Police chief Tim Huggins pledged, "Our goal will be to continue to offer the highest standard of professional services and to assure the safe and peaceful existence to all who live, work and shop in the city of Prattville."

Prattville Fire Engine Company

Daniel Pratt, William C. Allen, B.F. Miles, T.B. Avery, Samuel F. Ticknor and Ephraim S. Morgan, along with their associates and successors, were incorporated by the name Prattville Fire Engine Company on March 2, 1848. The company strove to instill character and responsibility in its members. The young men were charged with protecting the lives and property of their fellow citizens. This was a heavy burden, especially in the factory town, where a fire could destroy thousands of dollars' worth of property, take many lives and leave many people out of work.

Former Prattville fire chief Stanley Gann stated:

> *Daniel Pratt was one of the original founders of the Prattville Engine Company. Back then, they were a voluntary fire service, and they'd go around to businesses and collect dues. Insurance companies would sometimes pay homeowners-type insurance. There was a Hook and Ladder Company formed also as a separate company. I don't know how long the hook and ladder survived, but the Prattville Engine Company basically turned into the Prattville Fire Department as a volunteer department when the city incorporated.*

Pratt recalled that there were always some gin house fires. The picker room was located in the basement of the cotton mill. On June 28, 1854, the thermostat read ninety-seven degrees, and several bales of cotton ignited. The Fire Engine Company arrived in record time and easily extinguished the blaze. The pickery, a four-story building located next to the cotton mill, caught fire several years later. Although the Fire Engine Company was unable to save the structure, it did prevent the fire from spreading to other structures.

Fire Chief Stanley Gann

Former Prattville fire chief Stanley Gann recalled:

> *My dad had firemen friends in Montgomery, one in particular at Station Four on Bell Street. I played ball at the Boy's Club at West End. My mom worked at a shoe store on Dexter. When ball practice was over, I was told to go to the fire station on Bell Street and wait for my mom to pick me up. I got to know how a fire department worked. If the bell went off on the big red truck, I knew to step out of the way. Back then, Montgomery had all convertible trucks. They didn't have tops on them.*

The son of a military man, Stanley Gann was born in New Mexico but moved to Montgomery, Alabama, at four years old. In 1981, he submitted an application to both Montgomery and Prattville Fire Departments, but Prattville was quicker on the hiring process. Gann made chief in 1997. He noted:

> *In the late 1960s, they hired the first paid fire chief, which was Herman Scott. Donald McGough was the second paid person. At that point, they worked twenty-four hours on and twenty-four hours off, and they just started adding a few folks. The fire station was in the old city hall back then. They were located on the Chestnut Street side. The firemen were called by the siren on top of the building.*

A reception was held for Gann to celebrate his nearly thirty years of service to the city in March 2011. The sequence of events that led to his retirement began when Mayor Bill Gillespie called for his resignation after a statement Gann made to the television news about the impact that furloughs would have on the fire department. Terry Brown, a twenty-four-year veteran of the department, replaced Gann as fire chief.

Currently, the Prattville Fire Department serves a response area of thirty-six square miles, employs eighty full-time personnel (of whom fifty-five are nationally registered paramedics) and has three stations. As the only ambulance service in Autauga County, the department answers emergency and non-emergency calls, including non-emergency transports and contracts to respond to calls outside the city limits.

10

MAYORS AND NOTABLES

James Copeland Burns

Records indicate that Burns was the first person who was called by the title of mayor in Prattville. Daniel Pratt was, of course, the very first mayor of the town, but back then the term was "intendant." Intendant was used as a general term to refer to the holder of a public administrative office, and Pratt served as intendant from 1866 until his death in 1873. Burns was identified as intendant in the Code of 1896, and an article in the February 7, 1914 edition of the *Prattville Progress* refers to him as mayor.

A New York native, Burns came to Prattville about 1866 and was, for many years, a superintendent of the Daniel Pratt Gin Factory. Serving in the Civil War, he participated in many battles, including Gettysburg. At a time when the only salary for mayor was free water from the city, Burns was elected in that office four times and was serving the fourth term at the time of his death. Burns is listed as intendant from 1895 to 1897 and as mayor from 1902 to 1904, 1908 to 1910 and 1912 to August 1, 1915.

Old City Hall. *Courtesy of Rex Musgrove.*

Lewis N. Gillespie

Lewis N. Gillespie served a total of twenty years as mayor, from 1936 to 1952 and from 1956 to 1960. In 1936, the mayor and council members were elected by wards, and Gillespie won that year's election with a total of seventy-five votes.

The first matter of business for the officials in 1936 was the consideration of paving Chestnut Street from the intersection of Second Street (now Main Street) for a one-block distance. The reason given for paving was the possibility that a new post office would be built on the corner of Second and Chestnut Streets. The following is the city's financial standing for the first council meeting: $267.41 balance on hand; $2,841.16 collections during September; $1,228.43 disbursements for September; $1,880.14 balance October 1, 1936.

During Gillespie's tenure as mayor, many other streets were paved that previously had been dirt. Streets in the city were arranged so that they could be properly numbered and marked, and residents were required to properly

Downtown, looking from courthouse. *Courtesy of Rex Musgrove.*

Old Post Office. *Courtesy of Rex Musgrove.*

number and mark their residences and businesses. The first wastewater treatment plant was erected during Gillespie's administration. It was opened in 1959 and was located on Doster Road in the area now occupied by the Street and Vehicle Maintenance Departments.

When the senior center was built in May 1986, the city council passed a resolution to name it in Gillespie's honor. The center offers senior adults social interaction and activities that enhance quality of life, both physically and mentally.

Mac Gray

Former Prattville mayor Gray Price recalled, "Mac Gray was my wife Julie's uncle. People would get that name confused when I went into office because my first name is Gray."

Charles McDuffie "Mac" Gray served the citizens of Prattville as mayor from 1960 to 1980. According to family members, Gray liked to cook, and the following (more or less) is his Alabama Camp Stew recipe:

1 can Castleberry BBQ pork
1 can Castleberry BBQ beef or Lloyds BBQ pork and beef
1 large can Sweet Sue BBQ chicken, Lloyds BBQ chicken or just-pulled chicken (to be less sweet)
1 large can tomato sauce
2 cans diced tomatoes or fresh tomatoes
1 large onion, chopped
6 potatoes, peeled and cut
2½ tablespoons Worcestershire sauce (more if you'd like)
2 tablespoons lemon juice
1 teaspoon Tabasco Pepper Sauce (more if you'd like)
Salt and pepper to taste

In a big pot, add water, potatoes and add onions. Boil them until tender and then drain most of the water. Add the rest of the ingredients, keeping a few cups of liquid in the pot. Mix all ingredients in a large pot and simmer on low for two to three hours. Serve with hot cornbread.

Union Camp. *Courtesy of Alfred Wadsworth.*

Union Camp Corporation broke ground during Gray's administration in the spring of 1965, and the first roll of paper came off the paper machine in March 1967. In 1975, equipment was added to enable the use of recycled paper to generate new paper. Then, an expansion doubling the size of the mill (adding a second paper machine) started in 1978. In 1999, Union Camp merged with International Paper.

Mac Gray Park, named after the mayor, is located on Martin Luther King Jr. Drive across from the junior high school in Prattville. The park is the site of a softball complex, and the Autauga County Fair is held there every fall.

A Tale of Three Mayors on One Street

Tonight's News broadcast said that if Mayor Gillespie is not doing his job, Jim Byard knows how to find him because he lives just up the street from him. Everyone has always gotten some laughs from the fact that several mayors live in the same neighborhood.
—Jamie Hatfield Moncrief on the night before Bill Gillespie's swearing-in ceremony

Prattville native Bill Gillespie Jr. was sworn in as the city's mayor on January 18, 2011, after longtime mayor Jim Byard Jr. stepped down from his elected position to accept a position in Governor Robert Bentley's cabinet. Gillespie had previously served as the city council president.

The two certainly didn't have to travel far in order to congratulate each other since they live only a few houses apart on South Washington Street. If Bill should choose to seek out the wisdom of another former mayor for any reason, C. Gray Price, who was Prattville's city head from 1980 until 1992, also lives a very short distance from both Gillespie and Byard. All

Daniel Pratt Historic District. *Courtesy of Marc Parker.*

three families live in the Daniel Pratt Historic District, which is listed on the National Register of Historic Places in Alabama.

C. Gray Price

According to former mayor Gray Price, "Prattville was fairly small when I was elected. We had about twenty-one thousand people, and the east side was basically not developed to any degree. There was nothing past Kmart. But during my last two years, we tried to get all of that infrastructure out east."

Clarence Gray Price moved from North Carolina to Prattville in 1957 to live with his grandmother on Northington Street until he graduated high school. After that, Price entered the air force, serving active duty from 1961 until 1965. Admitting a lifelong interest in the operations of government, the former mayor would watch political conventions all night long on a black-and-white television set as a young man.

Price said, "I've always been interested in politics. I remember working for some guy running for governor when I was in the fifth or sixth grade. I think he got stomped. I ran around handing out pamphlets."

The former mayor's field of education, however, led him to the public school system, where he began an eleven-year career as a classroom teacher, assistant principal and principal. During his years as an educator, Price returned to college and earned an MS degree in administration/supervision from Troy State University in Montgomery:

> Some people talked me into running when I was principal in late 1976. I was going to run against a very popular person who had been on the council. I said, "You know, I'd like to do something for the city. If I win, I think I can help." If I didn't win, I was planning on maybe teaching history in college and go[ing] back [to] get my doctorate. It didn't work out that way.

Some of Price's accomplishments during his term of service include expansion of the sewer system, trying to get service industries to the city, remodeling the armory, street improvements, beginning the revitalization of downtown and erecting the senior center in 1986.

Mary Anne "Boo" Rogers, who, in almost twenty-five years, worked for three Prattville mayors (Gray Price, David Whetstone and Jim Byard Jr.) recalled:

Mayor Gray Price. *Courtesy of Alfred Wadsworth.*

Gray inherited Mayor Mac Gray's car to begin with when he became mayor, and it was this huge Crown Victoria. Gray was short, and when he got behind the wheel, you couldn't tell he was in there. They finally decided he needed a new car, so they bought him a used Lincoln Continental that was about a block long. It was yellow, and you could really see him coming down the street. One day, the chief of police [Alfred Wadsworth] and I decorated the car and pimped it up.

Price is also known for his sense of humor and acting ability. When the Montgomery Museum of Art was showing a collection of George Cooke's paintings, Price was asked to portray Daniel Pratt in a program held in the large rotunda. "Gray Price played the guard that had his feet up reading the paper in the film *The Traveling Executioner* that was filmed in the closed Kilby prison in Montgomery," Susan Cranfield remembered.

Old Prattvillage was established in 1982 during Price's administration. The historic area covers the first block of First Street and is on some of the land that Daniel Pratt purchased from Joseph May in 1835. The 1840 Mims Hotel was moved to Old Prattvillage. The main part of the hotel was saved, and it is listed on the National Register of Historic Places as a contributing property of the Daniel Pratt Historic District. According to Price, there were several other projects he had hoped to accomplish during his time in office: "One of the things I wanted to do, even though I'm an Auburn football fan, was to four lane Highway 82 to Tuscaloosa because of so many traffic deaths occurring there. It would also make it easier and quicker for students going back and forth to school."

From a meager budget of $3 million in 1980 during a recession when Price took office, he more than tripled the revenue in the 1992–93 budget. Upgrades of school buildings were made possible by his one-half-cent sales tax for education. A Kmart store was brought to the city, and some infrastructure was placed on the east side in order for growth to continue. Price wanted to bring more large industry to the city so that Prattville could be more self-sustaining and not rely so much on nearby Montgomery. He wanted to change the moniker that Prattville was a small, sleepy bedroom community.

Former Alabama state legislator Mac Gipson noted, "Gray was a good mayor. Prattville started growing beginning with Gray Price."

Price met his future wife, the former Julie Colley, when he first started teaching at the high school, and she was the secretary there. They knew each other because his uncle by marriage and Julie's mother were first cousins.

The former mayor retired from public office in October 1992, and in recognition of his professional achievements, the Alabama State Route 14 Bridge in downtown Prattville was named in his honor. This bridge is the former site of the old wool mill covered bridge over Autauga Creek, which, according to legend, was built by the slaves of Daniel Pratt. Price is currently an ombudsman at Central Alabama Aging Consortium, working as an advocate for residents in nursing homes and assisted living facilities.

David Whetstone Jr.

A native of Autauga County, David Whetstone Jr. became Prattville mayor in 1992 and was reelected in 1996. He also served two terms on the Autauga County Commission. For many purposes, such as allocating funds, the county commission is the governing body of the county. Whetstone provided leadership and support to numerous civic and professional organizations, including the Prattville Civitan Club, the Association of County Commissioners and the Autauga County Vocational Educational Advisory Council. The Robert Trent Jones Golf Trail project was endorsed by Whetstone and members of the city council during his term.

David Whetstone was a sitting mayor when he passed away at the age of fifty-six in June 1999 from a heart attack while in Germany. By Alabama law, the council president then becomes the mayor, and that position was held by Jim Byard Jr.:

> *I was getting ready for church, and the mayor's executive assistant told me I may hear there was an issue with the mayor, that he'd had a heart attack, was in the hospital and that she'd keep me updated. Monday afternoon I got a call from the city clerk saying I needed to come to city hall and that all council members were meeting there also. They didn't want me to make a statement to the press until after the 6:00 p.m. news because they were unsure if Mayor Whetstone's mom had been told. So, we waited, then had the police officers lower the flag and told the press the mayor had died, and in the interim I would become the mayor. I served the remainder of 1999. There was an election in August 2000. I ran and won.*

Jim Byard Jr.

Jim Byard's family moved to Prattville from Columbus, Georgia, when he was four years old because his father was a radio disc jockey at WPXC (PIXIE 1410) in the city. As far as Byard's taste in music goes, it ranges from the 1940s and big bands to hip hop, the '70s, Pink Floyd, the '80s funky sounds to Frank Sinatra, Elvis Presley, Willie Nelson and Dean Martin.

Graduating from Prattville High School, Byard worked for the local Kmart and a store called Aim For the Best that did not last long in the city, but there was politics in his blood. Crediting his grandfather's brother, Floyd Mann, for some of his political aspirations, Byard learned the basics of campaigning in 1980 while working at the city's Reagan headquarters and aiding Mann in the race for state treasurer in 1986.

Former Prattville High School teacher Susan Cranfield recalled:

*Jim was a wonderful student. He was politicking and didn't come to
class for his midterm. I told him I had to give him a take-home. Well,
Lord, he was incensed and wanted to know why I made him do it. I said,
"In the length of time it took to complain about this, you could have done
it three times!"*

Byard continued his education by earning a Bachelor of Arts degree in
political science with double minors in business and sociology from Troy
University in Montgomery. Having the education and a few years of political
experience under his belt, Byard ran for a seat on Prattville's city council
and was defeated on the first try. He was successful the next time, in 1992,
winning the district six seat. In 1998, Byard was elected again and voted
council president.

He recalled, "The police chief wanted to see my work permit because he
thought I was too young to be a city councilman. I was twenty-three years
old, and I looked twelve. I wore a bowtie back then, and that was the other
thing that everybody remembers about me."

The former mayor was two months shy of his thirty-third birthday when
he took office in June 1999 due to David Whetstone's untimely death, and
he was the youngest mayor in the city's history when elected the following
year, in 2000. One of his mentors, Fred Posey, the former Autauga County
circuit clerk, swore in the young man as mayor. Byard credits Posey with
teaching him that politics is a noble profession and can affect people's lives
in a positive way:

*I was young, so I probably would have done some things differently had I
had the eleven years experience as mayor. But I didn't have that experience
and relied heavily on senior staff. We had a flood that year. We were very
blessed with natural disasters.*

The former mayor cites his greatest accomplishments as streetscaping, the
investment in downtown Prattville and the historic district and helping to
bring the Navistar LPGA Classic tournament to the city. During his tenure as
Prattville's top official, the city experienced rapid growth and development,
with many retailers opening stores in the city, including Bass Pro Shops,
Publix and Best Buy. Byard served on the board of directors of the National
League of Cities and was president of the Alabama League of Municipalities
in 2004–2005. He is a founding board member of the Alabama Municipal
Funding Corporation. He is also proud of how the people reacted to the

2008 tornado, which wreaked havoc on the city, saying that as a whole, the response to the emergency was pretty impressive.

According to Byard's former secretary of ten years, Jamie Hatfield Moncrief, his genuineness was a great asset, as he always treated the oldest and the youngest citizens with the same sincerity, honestly caring about others' opinions and feelings. Moncrief said:

Jim has the most charisma of anyone I've ever met. I always joke and say, "If he wasn't a politician, he'd be a minister." One of my favorite things to do was to go to a school with Jim. Kids would see him and say, "There's the mayor!" Jim would sit in a tiny chair and tell them they were contributing to the city by buying a book or candy and that he works for them. He would put that Dr. Seuss hat on and look at each one of them eye to eye. We'd go to the senior center, and he'd pull the numbers for bingo. They just love him, but he loves them, too.

Autauga County circuit clerk Whit Moncrief recalled:

Jim loves people. He and I would go riding around to gas stations, find out-of-state tags and say, "Hey, thank you for coming to Prattville." They'd ask, "You're the mayor?" They wouldn't believe he'd be talking to them, so he'd whip out his ID and show them that he was the mayor. He just loved doing that.

Byard's entire eleven-plus years as mayor wasn't entirely free of bumps along the way, however. Prattville City Council members voted in October 2010 to borrow $3.1 million to satisfy a bond payment that provided millions of dollars for incentives to lure retail development to the east side of the city and to make capital improvements. After the vote, Byard was accused of being disingenuous with them, and it was decided that budget cuts should be implemented in order to provide the cash flow to pay the ongoing debt. In short, although the council members voted to approve the borrowing, they were dissatisfied with how things were handled.

About this, Byard said:

I'm human, but if you're involved in elected office, it's not a spectator sport. It's a contact sport, and you have to understand that going in. Leaders are different, and they have to lead. They can't punch. They have to take it. There are ways to disagree with honor and civility. I hope, in years to come,

Mayor Byard's last council meeting. *Courtesy of Marc Parker.*

people will remember I worked extremely hard, that I had a passion and that I loved the people of Prattville. I made mistakes, but in the overall scheme of things, I loved the city. I hope they think it's a better town because I served.

On January 12, 2011, during this third term, Mayor Jim Byard Jr. announced he would accept then governor-elect Robert Bentley's appointment to his cabinet as the director of the Alabama Department of Economic and Community Affairs (ADECA). He officially stepped down from his elected position as Prattville's chief executive officer at the close of business on Monday, January 17, 2011, assuming his new duties at ADECA the following day.

In this new position, Byard oversees a staff of more than two hundred and a budget of about $350 million annually. Working as an arm of the governor's office, ADECA awards hundreds of grants each year to city and county governments and nonprofit organizations. Communities across the state depend on ADECA funding to help with economic development, job training, law enforcement, energy conservation, recreation projects, community services and much more. Byard said:

We are the repository of federal dollars that come to the state. Governor-elect Bentley told me he wanted a mayor to lead ADECA because a mayor knows the value of what a federal dollar can do in his or her community.

I tell people that they may not know who the director of ADECA is, but the mayor knows, the probate judge knows and the county commission chairman knows because they count on us to help them with valuable necessary projects around the state. At some point, every citizen in Alabama has been touched by some project that ADECA has had a hand in. Projects in Prattville that are ADECA programs are the Wilderness Park, Upper Kingston Park, Pratt Pool and Canoe Trail.

Bill Gillespie Jr.

The man who took over Jim Byard's mayoral position is a businessman who has spent his entire life in Prattville. His family has owned an auto service and repair shop (Gillespie Tire & Automotive Service) in the city since 1955. Gillespie began in the business in 1970, taking over the management ten years later. His father, Bill Gillespie Sr., served on the Prattville City Council from 1984 until 1992, and Prattville's current head credits both his dad and the Dixie Youth League for his desire to enter public service:

I graduated high school in 1976 from Autauga County High School [now Prattville High School] *and attended several types of technical schools specializing in mechanics. I did some youth coaching and umpiring just to see what I could do to make a difference. I told my father that I was only interested in two terms on the city council, enough to maybe make things better in the city. I wasn't going to be a career politician, just go in and see what I could do, get out and then let somebody else step in.*

In 2004, following his father in the city's political circle, Gillespie was elected to serve district one on the city council, and he remained in that position for six years. He was voted by his peers to fill the position of council president pro tempore in December 2010. On January 14, 2011, he moved into the role of council president, but there was no time to get used to that position. Only four days later, Gillespie was sworn in as mayor of the city of Prattville when Jim Byard Jr. resigned. Gillespie noted:

I haven't seen my family as much since I've been mayor and haven't gotten as much sleep. Fortunately, my family is behind me, and many good staff

Mayor Bill Gillespie. *Courtesy of Marc Parker.*

and city members have helped me through the transition. I still have a lot to learn, but I feel comfortable. I think most of the city employees are comfortable with me.

The new mayor, having sat on the council bench for six years, already had some ideas he wanted to implement as mayor and chose to run the city similar to the operation of his tire business. He claims that his style of government is different than that of his predecessor:

Jim Byard is probably one of the best politicians I know. He's more polished than I am and speaks a lot better than me. I could say that I'm the mechanic and am here to give this city a tune-up! I'll be running it more by the numbers and will let the numbers tell us where we need to go. All departments are going to feel cuts, but the economy will hopefully turn around soon.

The new mayor requested an audit of the city's finances, and it revealed that Prattville's debt was more than $60 million and was still rising. The city council considered a budget proposal made by Gillespie, which included employee layoffs and furloughs in addition to a sales tax increase and a ten-dollar surcharge for sewer service. It was composed of expenditure reductions and revenue-generating processes. Gillespie said:

Before I stepped in, they had a lump-sum budget. We have now gone to a line-item budget, and the department heads are a lot more accountable. They have a standing order that any expenditure besides the normal day-to-day ones has to be approved by Doug Moseley [finance director] or me first. That has probably been one of the major changes. I'm doing my best not to micromanage, but at one point in time, our finance director told us if we did not do something, he projected a "crash and burn" would happen in the near future.

Former council president Dean Argo said of Gillespie:

I think Bill is a good guy and has a good heart. His dad was on the council, and his business is in Prattville, so Bill has a tremendous personal investment here. I think that he's not going to spend money and hire a bunch of people or take on any expensive projects, which will give the city time to regenerate to get the economy going again and get some money into reserve.

Wilson Pickett

Born in Prattville on March 18, 1941, Wilson Pickett became one of the most popular African American singers of the 1960s. The youngest of eleven children, Pickett's passionate style was nurtured in the Baptist choirs around Prattville. Pickett's hits include "In the Midnight Hour," "Mustang Sally," "Funky Broadway," "Land of a 1,000 Dances," "634-5789" and "She's So Good to Me." The impact of his songwriting and recording led to his 1991 induction into the Rock and Roll Hall of Fame.

According to Wilson Pickett's brother, Maxwell Pickett:

> *Wilson started singing at about eleven or twelve years old in the church, and our parents found out early on that he had a tremendous talent for singing, so they were in support of him, but they wanted him to remain in gospel. Of course, in those days, there wasn't a lot of money to be made in gospel, so he left and moved to Detroit to live with our father. While there, he was discovered by an R&B group named the Falcons. He signed with them, and the rest is history, as they say. His career just took off, and he left this world as an internationally loved artist.*

With many of Pickett's family members present, the City of Prattville honored the singer with a historical marker that was unveiled on December 8, 2009, at the Creative Arts House Garden located behind city hall. Former mayor Jim Byard Jr. announced at the gathering:

> *It is important that we pause and honor a native son of Prattville. Beginning as a youngster singing gospel music at local churches, to finding fame as a rhythm and blues artist, Wilson Pickett's music continues to be enjoyed by people of all ages.*

Maxwell Pickett and his sister, Louella New, traveled from Atlanta, Georgia, to attend the event honoring their famous brother. Wilson Pickett had two sons and two daughters: Michael Wilson, Saphan, Lynderrick and Veda Lynn Neal. The entire family has a deep-rooted history in the Fountain City.

Maxwell recalled:

> *We all worked on the farm in southwest Prattville, and whenever we'd get paid, we would come to Prattville to shop. I graduated from North*

Wilson Pickett Marker. *Courtesy of Marc Parker.*

Highland High School in the city and have great memories from great moments in Prattville. I remember that, early in his career, Wilson gave a concert at my school.

The famous singer was further recognized as the 2010 Fountain City Arts Festival's honoree. Pickett's career spanned over forty-five years. His musical breakthrough came with the recording of his third Atlantic single, "In the Midnight Hour." Also a talented songwriter, Pickett's songs were recorded by artists like Led Zeppelin, Van Halen, the Rolling Stones, Aerosmith, Credence Clearwater Revival and Bruce Springsteen, among others.

Roman Harper

Prattville native Roman Harper played quarterback, safety and returner for his hometown football team, the Lions, and led it to a 9-2 record his senior season. Harper continued in the sport at the University of Alabama, finishing his college career with 302 tackles, five interceptions, five forced fumbles, four fumble recoveries and three and a half sacks.

Roman Harper's childhood babysitter, Joanie Evans, recalled:

My boyfriend and I would take Roman and Ronnie to McDonalds when they were little. I got to know the family because Roman's dad was the coach when I was at Prattville High School. Roman was interested in football when he was four and would peek through the fence at the field to watch them play. He'd say, "I want to play," and I'd have to tell him that he was not old enough. Those two were just the sweetest boys.

Harper is currently a safety with the New Orleans Saints professional football franchise. In 2005, Hurricane Katrina devastated New Orleans, and the Superdome was used as an emergency shelter for displaced residents. The stadium suffered much damage from the disaster, and the Saints were forced to play some home games in other stadiums; however, the Superdome was repaired and renovated in time for the 2006 season. The Saints won their only Super Bowl championship during the 2009 season, defeating the AFC champion Indianapolis Colts 31–17.

Harper played a major role in the Saints' victory over Indianapolis in Super Bowl XLIV. He was the second-leading tackler on the team. Mayor Jim Byard Jr. proclaimed February 27, 2010, "Roman Harper Day" in the city, as several hundred New Orleans Saints fans flocked to the Doster Center to catch a glimpse of the star tackler and to take home a photo or autograph. The Saints safety signed T-shirts, footballs, helmets and posters for fans, posed for photographs and spoke about advice he would give to a young player just beginning his career:

> *Just work hard. I mean, have fun with it. Don't take it too seriously. Just go out there, and play the game for what it is. It's just a sport. At the end of the day, you've got to keep working, and if you want to make it into something, you've got to strive for it, and just go for it.*

The parents of the Saints player, Coach Ronald Harper and his wife, Princess, declare that there is always one of them attending each game. Princess shows her love by cooking her son's favorite dishes, which are consumed by not only Harper but also coaches and players alike. She said, "When we go to New Orleans, we don't go out. I cook macaroni and cheese, fried pork chops, creamed potatoes and steak and potato pies."

Kevin Turner

A 1987 graduate of Prattville High School, Kevin Turner is known in this part of the country for being a star fullback at the University of Alabama. He started forty-one consecutive games under Crimson Tide coaches Bill Curry and Gene Stallings and then went on to play professionally in 1992 for the New England Patriots and, in 1999, for the Philadelphia Eagles. His career ended when doctors diagnosed him with a narrowing of the spinal column.

In May 2010, after many tests and two surgeries to remove parts of his spine, Turner was diagnosed with amyotrophic lateral sclerosis (ALS), also referred to as Lou Gehrig's disease. Because he attributes this crippling disease to injuries he suffered in the National Football League, Turner is involved in research that links chronic traumatic encephalopathy (repeated brain trauma) in athletes to ALS. He suffered thousands of blows to the head and too many concussions to count during his football days. Through the Kevin Turner Foundation, he is raising awareness about these issues and bringing attention to the disease.

Turner doesn't believe the NFL has done enough to protect its players from these injuries, which could turn deadly, and believes the league should be forced into changing players' practice routines and generally taking steps to make the game safer. He feels that the NFL has, over the past couple decades, kind of turned a blind eye to the seriousness of not only concussions but also sub-concussive hits and the cumulative effects of them.

While it's not conclusive that Turner's injuries were caused by football, the forty-two-year-old believes there is a direct correlation between his former job and current condition. According to a recent report in the *Boston Globe*, Turner is the fourteenth NFL player to be diagnosed with ALS since 1960. The former athlete is now attached to a lawsuit intended to force the league into making the game safer.

11

BELIEVE IT OR NOT

Gurney Ghost

It was said that if you crossed the street in downtown Prattville by the Gurney building, you could see shadows going across the street. Even though the Gurney was destroyed by fire, some people say you can still see the shadows of people to this day. Before it burned down, folks reported seeing a woman who appeared to be searching for something. Legend has it that once in the 1920s, the entire night shift watched as she walked through the first-floor weaving room. Dozens of operators could be seen leaning out mill windows to watch the apparition glide across the creek and disappear from sight.

In the book *Jeffrey Introduces 13 More Southern Ghosts*, a Gurney night watchman related his story:

> *Don't laugh. I saw her as plain as I see you. It gives you the shivers. First time I saw her, I thought to quit my job, but she seemed harmless enough. She has been back three or four times. Always gives me a shock to step off the elevator or come up the stairs and see her walking straight and quiet along the rows of machines. She doesn't bother me, and I don't bother her.*

The woman is dressed in black and has been seen roaming between the rows of machines. It is speculated that she is looking for her son, ten-year-old Willie Youngblood, who was working in the third-floor spinning room when

Gin complex on a foggy night. *Courtesy of Marc Parker.*

he fell down a dusty elevator shaft in the lint-hazed cotton mill. His death left his mother alone, as his father had just died a few months earlier. She never recovered from the losses and died a year to the day that Willie was killed. The story goes that when the building burned in 2002, the only thing left standing was the elevator shaft.

Swept Away

Christy Burdett, owner of Vintage Blu, a consignment and gift shop in downtown Prattville, agrees that was rather strange when a run-of-the-mill $2.99 house broom could stand upright by itself. She doesn't think there is anything spooky about it, although several hundred people stopped by to view the oddity, and each one had his or her own opinion. Apparently, the broom loves just one spot on the store floor because people have moved it to other places and it has fallen. When it was moved back to its "favorite spot," the broom stood upright again. The owner brought in her toddler and asked him what he thought of the broom. He shivered and reported that there was cold air around the broom.

When Burdett posted about the phenomenon on Facebook, word spread quickly, and a paranormal group asked if it could check out the craziness. Southern Paranormal Researchers spent that Friday night at the store and didn't leave until two o'clock the next morning. The crew put teams in the store, in the basement and in the building next door, which houses Lucky Photography. The basement team thought it had some shadow movement and felt the presence of several spirits; the lights flickered next door; and some members of the team just generally had the feeling of a creepy presence.

As word got out, folks stopped by Vintage Blu to share their own downtown ghost stories. The owner of Lucky Photography told her that he didn't want to mention this when she moved in, but *he* had a broom that would stand up by itself. He couldn't reveal that to his partner because she was scared of ghosts. A local attorney, George Walthall, owns the building, and the girls who work for him talk about the times they see an older man and woman upstairs. He had no explanation for the "magic" positioning of the broom: "I had a client a long time ago that was into voodoo, but, that's been a long time ago. If there are any spirits in the building, I'll just send them downstairs."

Mysterious Shadows and Sounds at Buena Vista

Southern Paranormal Researchers, the same "ghost busting" group that investigated the standing broom phenomenon, checked out the beautiful antebellum home called Buena Vista, which has long been rumored to be haunted. The house was built in the early 1820s by one of the first landowners, but construction was not completely finished until North Carolina native Captain William Montgomery assumed ownership. Through several changes of ownership, the home has gone through two construction styles—Federal and Greek revival (adding the Ionic columns). One of the outstanding features of the interior is the circular mahogany staircase that spirals twenty-four feet to the third floor. An expanded design of the staircase was used when the capitol was built in Montgomery, Alabama.

During the paranormal investigation on the second floor, whispers were detected, and a loud child's voice was heard to say, "Momma." Shadows were seen moving through the second-floor bathroom, and unexplained cold spots were picked up throughout the home. A full-bodied apparition of a man walking from the hallway into the office was seen. Music resembling 1920s jazz was playing somewhere upstairs to the point that it was thought someone had turned on the radio. Apparently, the caretakers of the home hear this music on a fairly regular basis.

Behind the home, there are a few graves, but only two or three are marked, and a couple of them appear to be of the Montgomery family. This is the area where the researchers picked up the presence of a man, and at that very instant, a large tree limb suddenly fell from a nearby tree. The EVP (electronic voice phenomenon) captured two thumps, like someone was hitting the tree, just before the limb fell. The presence of a woman who had been shot, fell out of a second-story window and was secretly buried was felt. This story, oddly enough, had been heard before but had not been shared beforehand with the paranormal researchers.

Naturally, as investigators, the paranormal researchers search for hard evidence to support their individual personal experiences (the team comprised eleven members). The final verdict was that there *is* paranormal activity at Buena Vista largely caused by the residual energy within the home and outside property. They could not say, based on the evidence, if there is any intelligent spirit activity there, unless the statement caught on EVP that said, "Get out right now," is accurate. In that case, this might indicate an intelligent presence. There were many "ifs" to point one way or another, but it was definitely felt that there is some sort of paranormal activity going on, intelligent or not.

Buena Vista is operated and maintained by the Autauga County Heritage Association and was the first Autauga County entry to the National Register of Historic Places (in 1974). The grounds are available for tours, weddings and personal or corporate events. Visitors can step back in history, enjoy the parlor and the antiques and dream of antebellum balls, while quite possibly experiencing a visit from "beyond the grave."

The Ghost of Daniel Pratt

We dare say that an occasional visitor to the gin factory at night could have seen a light or an apparition that he believed to be the ghost of the town's founding father himself, but to our knowledge, there have been no documented cases of an actual ghost of Daniel Pratt. There is, however, a progressive pop/rock group, formed in 2008, of the same name.

The founding members, Brandon Wise and Jesse Livingston, began writing for fun in Livingston's Montgomery apartment. Now, the guys write songs that have been inspired by friends from high school and their hometown of Prattville. The musicians of the Ghost of Daniel Pratt (GDP) are Brandon Wise (guitar, vox, keys), Jesse Livingston (tables, vox) and Spencer Oates (bass guitar). GDP booked its first live show in June 2012 in Birmingham, Alabama. The band writes on its Facebook page:

> *I guess we found our writing niche due to the fact that everyone has a story or something that happened to them in their past. Now, we have close to twenty original songs pertaining to these "life stories" or life situations. We don't hold anything back, even when a song's lyrics are about ourselves. Every song has a story, I guess, and we tell it in our own crazy, surprising and metaphorical way.*

12

PRATTVILLE TODAY
AND BEYOND

The future of the Fountain City has much to do with its people. These are hardworking, Christian folks, many of whom loved Prattville just as much when it was a town of merely 18,647 in 1980 as they do now, in 2012, when the population has almost doubled in size. The city has been slowly moving away from being a "bedroom community" of Montgomery because of the diverse shopping and eating establishments that have settled in the area, and it most certainly will continue to do so in the upcoming years.

Dean Argo noted:

I never liked the term "bedroom community" because it always kept us in the shadow of Montgomery even though I know 60 percent of our workforce works in Montgomery. I really think when Jim [Byard] was mayor and through the city council from 2000 to 2008, we collectively really moved Prattville to a totally separate place standing on its own, doing things even Montgomery wished they could have done, and it took us out of that "suburb of" place. I always thought that term downgraded Prattville.

I think that people were so used to Prattville being a small town that when we began to grow in the late 1990s, the younger people saw that as something wonderful, but the older generation grew up thinking that everything you wanted, you had to go to Montgomery. As that started to change, it was good for them, but they didn't want Prattville to lose its small-town feel. We knew we'd never be able to spend as much money as Montgomery has on shops and industry, so we had to talk about our close-

Gin complex. *Courtesy of Marc Parker.*

knit neighborhoods, our schools and low crime rate to establish our own identity and goals.

Just as Daniel Pratt and the town's early pioneers came together to work toward a common goal in the 1800s, Prattville's residents united through the years in times of heartache and happiness. An example of the community working together in the summer of 2012, from the mayor on down to the average citizen, was when it accomplished the impossible by garnering enough votes to crown Pratt Park "America's Favorite Park." Coca-Cola sponsored the contest, and Prattville handily won by a wide margin over second-place finisher Krull Park in Olcott, New York, receiving a $100,000 grant to be used to help restore, rebuild or enhance the activity area in Pratt Park. The City of Prattville chose to use the money toward a splash pad project.

Mayor Bill Gillespie recalled:

When we took on this challenge, we promised the people of Prattville that we would use the grant funds to install a splash pad in Pratt Park. Our residents contacted their families and friends all over the country. We had an outpouring of support like nothing we had ever experienced. We thank Coca-Cola wholeheartedly for the opportunity they provided our community with this contest. While winning the grant was our goal, the most valuable reward was the way our community came together, worked hard together, and the feeling of pride and ownership that resulted from our efforts.

International Paper Company, which opened as Union Camp in 1967, is the largest employer in the city, and smaller industries related to plastics, automotive industry–related manufacturing, packing and power generation have opened. Many Prattville citizens work outside the city, primarily in Montgomery because the city is a mere fifteen minutes away from the downtown Montgomery state departments and Maxwell Air Force Base. Autauga County continuously grows in population, as does the state of Alabama.

According to a *Montgomery Advertiser* article in February 2011:

Autauga County had the biggest percentage of population increase, growing by nearly twenty five percent since 2000 from 43,671 to 54,571. The state's population keeps inching toward five million with a 7.5% increase since 2000 to 4,779,736. Since 1990, a significant portion of the growth in Autauga County has been in and surrounding the city of Prattville. Between 1990 and 2000, the city's population grew by 24.1% to 24,303.

City planner Joel Duke noted:

Prattville's growth in the last fifteen years has been caused partially by migration from Montgomery but partly also on overall growth in the region, with people being attracted here. Prattville is not growing that much today. There were two large growth spurts—one in the 1980s and one in the late 1990s, which continued into the 2000s. But workers tend to migrate to Prattville because of the amenities that are offered, the lifestyle and the housing. I think there's a possibility to see some synergy between downtown Montgomery and East Prattville, where there could be some office growth.

The city covers approximately twenty-four square miles of area, and according to the 2010 census, there are about thirty-four thousand people living there. One can imagine Daniel Pratt's vision for Prattville while visiting downtown Heritage Park and staring into the falling waters of

Clock tower. *Courtesy of Marc Parker.*

Heritage Park. *Courtesy of Marc Parker.*

A Brief History of the Fountain City

Autauga Creek against the backdrop of his former gin factory. Many out-of-town visitors are attracted to the Robert Trent Jones Golf Trail and to the shopping in downtown and East Prattville, among other locations.

Former Prattville Chamber of Commerce president Jeremy Arthur said:

> *Our Chamber is not a "mom and pop" one that you find in smaller cities that plan socials, teas and parades. We have our own board, and we are classified as a 501(c)(6), so it's a business nonprofit, but different than a charity. You wouldn't see a lot of communities step out on a limb and recruit a golf course. That happened two years before I got here. Over 100,000 rounds are played at the Robert Trent Jones Golf Trail each year, 60,000 of which are played by out-of-towners. I just finished up the cost analysis for the LPGA. Our $200,000 investment has a $7 million return. That's direct. Indirectly, it is $21 million.*

Prattville is still known today as the "Birthplace of Industry in Alabama" because Pratt's gin company became the foremost producer of cotton gins in the world. This is a city that blends the small-town quaintness and charm of a rich, historic past with a culture and a progressiveness all its own. Preservation is a major part of Prattville's heritage nowadays, with the renovation of the historically significant Continental Gin buildings.

To further remember the significant contribution Prattville's founder made in the world of manufacturing and commercial enterprise, the Alabama Department of Archives and History wishes to place a Daniel Pratt–produced cotton gin in a new exhibit that will deal with the role cotton played in the antebellum period and beyond. The city council passed a resolution approving the gin (formerly located at city hall) to be loaned to the archives for ten years.

Councilman Albert Striplin stated:

> *I've talked to the Prattaugan Museum and the Autauga County Heritage Association. There is a great interest in having the gin displayed at the Archives building. It would be a good way to tell the story of Daniel Pratt and the role Prattville has played in the industrialization of the state and region.*

We would like to end this short history book with just a few comments from the people who live in Prattville and the reasons why they love "The Fountain City":

The company I was with moved me from Omaha, Nebraska, down South. They told me that as long as I worked close to an airport where I could fly where I needed to be, they didn't care where I lived. So we shopped around in Georgia, Mississippi and Alabama. We chose Prattville because we found the people to be very warm and welcoming. I guess I decided to run for council because I felt (and still feel) that I owed a great debt to the people for embracing us when we first came here.
—Former city council president Mike Renegar

We moved here when I was ten in 1978. For the most part, I grew up here and was raised here. I went off to college, came back home and actually married my high school sweetheart. We are raising our kids here. People are coming to Prattville because they know their kids can get a good education. I've been fully pleased with the school system.
—Former city councilman Nathan Fank

I had the good fortune of playing at Daniel Pratt's house when I was in junior high school. Of course, I didn't appreciate all of that then. The old Northington home looked like a castle. My friends lived underneath it in sort of an old hole-in-the-wall with a heater. Prattville was a good place to grow up.
—Retired Prattville schoolteacher Susan Cranfield

When I worked for Mayor Jim Byard, we [the staff] *were really close. I was both secretary and administrative assistant, so it was me, Gina and Stephanie. The two of them had been working together for twenty-one years. It was just the three of us and the mayor. Beverly* [Byard] *had just given birth to their first son. We were walking out of the hospital after going to visit. Someone asked, "Well, hello Mayor, what are you doing here?" Jim said, "Our wife just had a son!" We were close-knit. I was blessed with that job because of the closeness and because I love this town.*
—Former secretary to Mayor Jim Byard and Mayor Bill Gillespie, Jamie Hatfield Moncrief

I came to Prattville the week after I graduated from Alabama, and I had a job with the Extension Service. My mom came with me, and we were going to look for an apartment. There were three rooms in Prattville available. Elmore's used to be the Dime Store, where the antique shop is now. We pulled around that corner, and there was no more town. I cried and cried.

There were less than four thousand people here then. I said I'd never marry a farmer. I married a farmer, and I'm still here.
—Former secretary to three mayors, Mary Anne "Boo" Rogers

I think we've made good advances on giving people something to ride, walk on and get exercise. The city owns about sixty-two and a half acres off Main Street, and my hope is that we could have four or five trails, maybe a hiking trail, a bicycling trail, a mountain bike trail and maybe an equestrian trail. If this happens, I think we may have a big influx of people coming in, setting up residence here. If not, they can come in and eat, buy gas and enjoy what Prattville has to offer. I'd like to be remembered after my time in office as the guy who left it better than he found it. If I'm not sitting in this green chair after August, I'll be back at my "Mayberry" tire store and playing more golf.
—Mayor Bill Gillespie

The incumbent mayor is indeed still reclining in his green chair after winning his first elected full term, with just under 70 percent of the vote, on August 28, 2012. In a news story, Gillespie stated that he believes the citizens of the city want to give him a chance to finish what he started:

The city of Prattville is ready to come together. I appreciate the confidence the voters have placed in me to lead this city for another term. Prattville has some good times ahead. We just have to continue to work hard to get there.

BIBLIOGRAPHY

Books and E-Books

Aiken, Boone. *Will Howard Smith and McQueen Smith Farms*. Unknown binding, 1971.

Armes, Ethel. *The Story of Coal and Iron in Alabama*. Cambridge, UK: University Press, 1910.

Bragg, William Harris. *Griswoldville*. N.p.: Mercer University Press, 2009.

Britton, Karen Gerhardt. *Bale o' Cotton: The Mechanical Art of Cotton Ginning*. College Station: Texas A&M University Press, 1992.

Burnett, Jason. *Bessemer*. Images of America. Charleston, SC: Arcadia Publishing, 2011.

Causey, Donna R. *Biographies of Notable & Some Not-So-Notable Alabama Pioneers*. Vol. 6. Amazon Digital Services, 2012.

DuBose, Joel Campbell. *Notable Men of Alabama: Personal and Genealogical*. Vol. II. Atlanta, GA: Southern Historical Association, 1904.

Evans, Curtis J. *The Conquest of Labor: Daniel Pratt and Southern Industrialization*. N.p.: Louisiana State University Press, 2001.

Ford, Arthur Peronneau. *Life in the Confederate Army: Being Personal Experiences of a Private Soldier in the Confederate Army; and Some Experiences and Sketches of Southern Life*. N.p.: Neale Publishing Company, 1905.

Franklin, Patrick Cooke. *Daniel Pratt: The Milledgeville Houses*. N.p.: University of Georgia Press, 2000.

Gillespie, Michele. *Free Labor in an Unfree World: White Artisans in Slaveholding Georgia, 1789–1860*. N.p.: University of Georgia Press, 2004.

Griffith, Lucille. "A Day with Daniel Pratt." In *Alabama: A Documentary History to 1900*. Tuscaloosa: University of Alabama Press, 1972.

Henderson, Aileen Kilgore. *Eugene Allen Smith's Alabama: How a Geologist Shaped a State*. N.p.: New South Books, April 1, 2011.

Hutto, Richard Jay. *Jordan Massee: Accepted Fables*. N.p.: Indigo Custom Publishing, 2005.

Ingham, John N. *Biographical Dictionary of American Business Leaders*. Vol. 1. N.p.: Greenwood Publishing Group, 1983.

Jefferson County Historical Commission. *Birmingham and Jefferson County*. Images of America. Charleston, SC: Arcadia Publishing, 1998.

Lakwete, Angela. *Inventing the Cotton Gin: Machine and Myth in Antebellum America*. N.p.: JHU Press, 2003.

Lewis, Walter David. *Sloss Furnaces and the Rise of the Birmingham District*. N.p.: University Alabama Press, 1994.

Lupold, John S., and Thomas L. French Jr. *Bridging Deep South Rivers: The Life and Legend of Horace King*. N.p.: University of Georgia Press, 2004.

MacDonald, Lois. *Southern Mill Hands: A Study of Social and Economic Forces in Certain Textile Mill Villages*. New York, 1928.

Martin, Gay N. *Alabama Off the Beaten Path*. 8th ed. N.p.: GPP Travel, 2006.

Massey, John. *Reminiscences: Giving Sketches of Scenes Through which the Author Has Passed and Penportraits of People Who Have Modified His Life*. N.p: University of California Libraries, 1916.

Matthews, Mrs. Pitt Lamar. *History Stories of Alabama*. Dallas, TX: Southern Publishing Company, 1920.

McWhorter, Diane. *Carry Me Home: Birmingham, Alabama: The Climactic Battle of the Civil Rights Revolution*. 2nd ed. New York: Simon and Schuster, 2002.

Miller, Randall M. *The Cotton Mill Movement in Antebellum Alabama*. N.p.: Ohio State University, 1971.

Mims, S. *Hon Daniel Pratt: A Biography with Eulogies on His Life and Character*. Edited by Mrs. S.F.H. Tarrant. N.p.: Whittet & Shepperson Publishers and Printers, 1904.

Mims, Wilbur F. *War History of the Prattville Dragoons*. N.p.: Eastern Digital Resources, 1999

Owen, Thomas McAdory, and Marie Bankhead Owen. *History of Alabama and Dictionary of Alabama Biography*. N.p.: S.J. Clarke Publishing Company, 1921.

Penhald, Ken, and Martin Everse. *Helena*. Images of America. Charleston, SC: Arcadia Publishing, 1998.

Rhyne, Jennings Jefferson. *Some Southern Cotton Mill Workers and Their Villages*. Chapel Hill: University of North Carolina Press, 1930.

Ruggles, Clifton, and Olivia Rovinescu. *Outsider Blues: A Voice from the Shadows*. N.p.: Fernwood Publishing, 1996.

Seay, Solomon S., Jr., with Delores R. Boyd. *Jim Crow and Me: Stories from My Life as a Civil Rights Lawyer*. N.p.: New South Books, 2008.

Thornton, J. Mills, II. *Politics and Power in a Slave Society: Alabama, 1800–1860*. N.p.: Louisiana State University Press, 1978.

Utz, Karen R. *Sloss Furnaces*. Images of America. Charleston, SC: Arcadia Publishing, 2009.

Wells, Jonathan Daniel. *The Origins of the Southern Middle Class, 1800–1861*. Chapel Hill: University of North Carolina Press, 2004.

Windham, Katherine Tucker. *Jeffrey Introduces 13 More Southern Ghosts*. Tuscaloosa: University of Alabama Press, 1987.

Magazines

DeBow, James Dunwoody Brownson. *DeBow's Review*. Published monthly in New Orleans, 1846–1884

Interview with Alexis "Lexi" Thompson: "An American Wunderkind." *Smashing Interviews Magazine* (September 6, 2012).

"Spotlight on Prattville & Autauga County." *Business Alabama Monthly* (May 1996).

Manuscript Collections

Malcolm C. McMillan Papers. Auburn University Archives, Auburn, AL.

Newspapers

Albany Herald. "Life in the South Different Before Civil Rights Movement." October 23, 2011.

Athens Banner-Herald. "Atlanta Firm Eyes Historic Mill for Development." April 2, 2012.

Biloxi Daily Herald. "Flood Area in Alabama Is Evacuated." August 18, 1939.

Gadsden Times. "Brown Slated as Witness in Prattville." October 19, 1967.

———. "Coroner Investigates Brother's Fatal Wreck." March 31, 1991.

Mexia Weekly Herald. "Alabama Town Under Water." August 18, 1939.

Montgomery Advertiser, May 14, 1873; February 25, 2011; May 12, 2011; January 15, 2012; March 20, 2012.

———. "Deluge in Downtown Prattville." May 7, 2009.

———. "Early Pastor Once President Garfield's Classmate." January 20, 2009.

———. "ESPN in Prattville: High School Football on a Big Stage." September 26, 2009.

———. "Gillespie Elected to Full Term in Prattville," August 29, 2012.

———. "Gin Co. a Blast During WW II, August 9, 2012.

———. "Historical Marker Brings Wilson Pickett's Family to Prattville." December 2, 2009.

———. "'Interview' with Daniel Pratt." May 6, 2009.

———. "LPGA Star Natalie Gulbis Tosses Game Coin as the Lions Roar." October 3, 2009.

———. "New Orleans Saints' Roman Harper Celebrated in Prattville." February 27, 2010.

———. "Prattville Officials Begin Budget Work." June 26, 2012.

———. "State Archives Wants to Display Pratt Cotton Gin," August 9, 2012.

———. "Tornado Slams Prattville; 200+ Homes Damaged." February 18, 2008.

Our Prattville—A News Magazine. "The Autauga County Fair Opens." September 23, 2008.

———. "Wilson Pickett's Brother Speaks About His Family." July 8, 2009.

Prattville Progress. Miscellaneous 1929 ads and articles. Autauga County Heritage Center.

———. "Prattville: Our Town, USA." August 25, 1966.

Sarasota Herald-Tribune. "Creek Rises." August 16, 1939.

Southern Advocate. "Present Position of Alabama." Letter from Daniel Pratt.
Southern Courier. "Citizens Protest Rasberry Death." February 25–26, 1967.
———. "For the People of Prattville." June 17–18, 1967.
———. "White Jury Frees Negro." March 30–31, 1968.
Times Daily. "Prattville Negro is on Trial." March 20, 1968.
Tuscaloosa News. "Boycott Fails in Prattville." February 20, 1967.
———. "Carmichael and Brown Want Out of Prattville Police Suit." August 11,1967.
———. "Five Teens Sentenced for Prattville Mill Fire." December 8, 2002.
———. "Prattville Will Help Itself: Town Maps Program for Flood Control After Plea Fails." September 26, 1940.

Papers/Reports/Pamphlets/Periodicals

Alabama Historical Quarterly. State at Large, 1878–1879.
Annual Report of the State Board of Health of Alabama, 1883–84. N.p.: Barrett & Co., 1885.
Autauga County Heritage Association. *Buena Vista.*
Cain, Nelda. "Bert and Dan...and the Ku Klux Klan." N.d.
———. *North Highland High.* Edited by Susan Bateman Cranfield. N.d.
Griffin, Richard W. "Cotton Manufacture in Alabama to 1865." *Alabama Historical Quarterly* (Fall 1956).
Medical Association of the State of Alabama: The Report of the State Board of Health. 1881.
Mims, Shadrack. "History of Autauga County." *Alabama Historical Quarterly* (Fall 1946).
Nobles, Larry N. With help from Eugene Thomas's grandson. *Prathoma.*
"Prattville & Autauga County Promo." *Business Alabama Monthly* (1996).
Price, C. Gray. Paid political advertisement literature.
Rogers, Mary Anne "Boo." "Intendants, Mayors, Council Members, City of Prattville, Alabama." N.d.
"The Siege at Prattville." *Movement* 3, no. 7 (July 1967).

Websites

Abney Family. www.shadylnfarm.com.

Alabama Archives Project. www.files.usgwarchives.net.

"Alabama Cotton Producer Jimmy Sanford is Recipient of Cotton Service Award," February 1, 2001. www.cotton.org.

Alabama Facts. Autauga County Information. www.encyclopediaofalabama.org.

Alabama Fuel & Iron Company Letter from Charles F. DeBardeleben. www.acumen.lib.ua.edu.

Alabama Historical Association Markers, Confederate Military Unit Histories. www.archives.alabama.gov.

"Alabama's RTJ Golf Trail Provides a True Test," February 22, 2010. www.golfweek.com.

"ALS Sufferer Kevin Turner Explains Why He's Suing NFL," June 7, 2012. www.insidetheiggles.com.

"American Civil War: The Soldier's Life." www.thomaslegion.net.

"Anderson Takes Over at Prattville," February 22, 2012. www.thewetumpkaherald.com.

"April's Fury: An Intimate Journal," August 21, 2011. www.myfoxal.com.

Auburn Research and Technology Foundation Board of Directors: James Sanford. www.auburnresearchpark.com.

Autauga County High School, Stanley Jensen Stadium. Old Prattvillage Census Info. www.prattvilleal.org.

"Autauga County in the Civil War." www.autaugaatwar.com.

"Autauga County Remembers Long Time Circuit Clerk," December 4, 2007; "Prattville Storm Now Identified as Category EF3 Tornado," February 19, 2008; "Prattville City Council Approves Proposal to Borrow $3.1 Million," October 26, 2010; "Prattville Audit Shows Deep Debt Load," February 22, 2011; "Prattville Fire Chief Stanley Gann Honored at Retirement," May 24, 2011. www.wsfa.com.

Bio of Samuel Parrish Smith. www.usarchives.net.

Boutin, Guy. "Story of the Gurney Fire." www.bamarider.com.

"Brown, Burt, Abney, Watts, and Related Families." www.freepages.genealogy.rootsweb.ancestry.com.

Buena Vista Plantation, July 25, 2009. www.southernparanormalresearchers.com.

Census Info. www.alabamagenealogy.com.

Churches in Prattville. www.churchangel.com

City Information. www.prattvilleal.gov.

"City of Prattville v. Corley, et al." October 10, 2003. www.findlaw.com.

Civil War Message Board. www.history-sites.com.

Daniel Pratt Cotton Mill Fire. www.rkmcall.com/ginfire.

Daniel Pratt's family. www.newsarch.rootsweb.com.

Daniel Pratt; Prattville, AL; New Orleans Saints; Kevin Turner. www.wikipedia.org.

"Death & Marriage Notices from Missing Issues of Autauga County Newspapers." www.rootsweb.ancestry.com.

"Descendants of Peter Wiley Kerlin." www.familytreemaker.genealogy.com.

Early Prattville, Autauga County, AL. www.alabamapioneers.com.

"Final Round Recap," 2011. www.navistarlpgaclassic.com.

"Former Alabama Running Back Kevin Turner Has ALS and Why That Matters So Much," August 20, 2010. www.rollbamaroll.com. Genealogy Info. www.africanheritage.com.

"Golf Courses Drive Area's Economic Development, October 1, 2000." www.americancityandcounty.com.

"Good Health to All From Rexall: History of Rexall." www.capnrexall.blogspot.com.

Griswold & Gunnison Revolver. www.vincelewis.net.

Griswoldville. www.georgiaencyclopedia.org.

"Griswoldville, Georgia—Industry and War in the Old South." www.exploresouthernhistory.com.

Gurney Building, Prattville, Alabama. www.strangeusa.com.

"Gurney Manufacturing Company: Prattville, Alabama." www.unsolvedmysteries.com.

Henry DeBardeleben. www.hooveral.org.

"High Point Sells for $33.8 Million." www.thewetumpkaherald.com.

History of Autauga County. July 2012 Newsletter (plans for redevelopment of Pratt's manufacturing complex). www.autaugaheritage.org.

"History of Continental Eagle." www.coneagle.com (now defunct).

"History of Drugstores." www.drugstoremuseum.com.

History of Milledgeville, Georgia. www.milledgevillega.us.

History of Prattville, Alabama. www.pratthistory.com (now defunct).

"Houser v. Hill," January 16, 1968. www.findacase.com.

Information on Churches. www.visithistoricprattville.com.

Information on Prattville Dragoons. www.theprattvilledragoons.blogspot.com.

Jim Byard Jr. www.governor.alabama.gov.

Kevin Turner Foundation. www.kevinturnerfoundation.org.

"Kevin Turner, Suffering from ALS, Explains Why He's Suing the NFL," June 7, 2012. www.profootballtalk.nbcsports.com. Mac Gipson. www.ballotpedia.org.

Mac Gray's Camp Stew Recipe (donated to website from a family member). www.laramielive.com.

"Marlor Presented the Face of Antebellum Milledgeville." www.unionrecorder.com.

"Mayor Gillespie Announces Re-Election Bid," April 17, 2012. www.prattville.wsfa.com.

Merrill Pratt's Gin at Auburn, AL. www.wireeagle.auburn.edu.

Milledgeville, Georgia. www.triposo.com.

News 2012. www.prattvillechamber.com.

Obituary of Daniel Pratt Jr. www.newspaperarchive.com.

"Planning Prattville Into the 21st Century, Inventory of Physical Conditions." www.projectprattville.com.

Prattmont Drive-In. www.cinematreasures.org.

Prattville, Alabama. www.cicotello.com.

"Prattville, AL's High Point Town Center on Auction Block Thursday," June 28, 2011. www.commercialbrokerblog.com.

"Prattville, AL: Serious Tornado Damage," February 18, 2008. www.blogspot.com.

Prattville Dragoons. www.jjoakley.com/dragoonhistory.html.

Prattville High School Sports and Athletics. "Jamey Dubose Departs Prattville," February 2, 2012. www.ihigh.com.

"Prattville Lions are Serious Business," July 23, 2011. www.espn.go.com.

Prattville Lodge history. "Coca-Cola Announces Pratt Park Is America's Favorite Park." www.prattvillelodge.org.

"Prattville Mayor Bill Gillespie Elected to First Full Term," August 28, 2012. www.wncftv.com.

"Prattville Mayor Says City Has Made Great Strides in Reducing Debt," February 23, 2012; "Prattville Fire, Police Chief Positions Filled," September 8, 2011. www.blog.al.com.

"Prattville Police Chief Retires After 40 Years of Service," March 30, 2011. www.wakacbs8.com.

"Remembering the Prattville Tornado." www.activerain.com.

"Robert Trent Jones Golf Trail." www.golfdigest.com.

Robert Trent Jones Golf Trail at Capitol Hill, Prattville. "Golf World Raves About Alabama's RTJ Golf Courses: Opelika and Prattville Sites Rank #1 & #2, Mobile #32," February 2009; "History of the Trail." www.rtjgolf.com.

Roney, Marty. "Bill Would Allow Cameras in Patient Rooms." March 22, 2009. www.alada19.com.

———. "Murder Shakes Alabama Town 10 Years Later," August 15, 2011. www.usatoday.com.

———. "Standing Broom Has Folks Here Strawstruck." *Montgomery Advertiser*, August 26, 2009. www.southernparanormalresearchers.com.

Samuel Griswold. www.griswoldfamily.org.

Save the Daniel Pratt Gin Factory. The Ghost of Daniel Pratt. www.facebook.com.

Sign on Autauga Creek. www.waymarking.com.

"Surveillance Cameras Capture Prattville Tornado on Tape," February 18, 2008. www.wistv.com.

"Wall Street Lawyer Goes South," Stokely Carmichael in Prattville June 1967. www.donjelinek.com.

Williams-Orme-Crawford-Sallee Home in Milledgeville, Georgia. www.historicantebellumhomes.wordpress.com.

ABOUT THE AUTHORS

Although born in Montgomery, Alabama, computer scientist and web pioneer MARC PARKER has deep ancestral roots in the Prattville community and has lived in the River Region most of his life. He has attended Auburn University and Harvard University, with major studies in English and computer science. Marc has had a lifelong love of music and was a professional singer/songwriter from the age of eighteen to his mid-twenties. He is a longtime licensed amateur radio operator and is presently an artist and a professional photographer.

A retired State of Alabama employee, MELISSA PARKER is also a native of Montgomery; she attended Troy University with major studies in criminal justice and psychology. Melissa has always been interested in writing and has created crossword puzzles that have been published in *Penny Press* and *Dell* magazines. She was also a tennis instructor at a country club in Montgomery in her twenties.

While living in Prattville during 2005, the husband-and-wife team created *Our Prattville—A News Magazine*, a media organization that covered local, state and national news, as well as featured sports, travel, history, lifestyles, entertainment articles and original, in-depth, industry-wide entertainment interviews. The two journalists covered major news events and press conferences statewide. In September 2010, the duo was contacted by The History Press and was asked to write the first nationally published book on the history of Prattville, Alabama.

Two years ago, Marc and Melissa branched off from *Our Prattville* and founded *Smashing Interviews Magazine* (smashinginterviews.com), which is international in scope, and primarily features original interviews from all genres—i.e., actors, athletes, authors, businesspeople, comedians, designers, directors, journalists, musicians, newsmakers, photographers and scientists.

Smashing Interviews Magazine has been quoted and cited in *TV Guide*, the *Atlantic Monthly* and on CBS and FOX television websites, as well as in numerous other publications. In the acting category, interviews include legends Ernest Borgnine, George Kennedy, Carol Channing and George Lindsey; Academy Award–winner Timothy Hutton; the storied British talent Malcolm McDowell; multiple award–winners Sharon Gless and Tyne Daly; Michael Rooker of *The Walking Dead*; Stephen Lang of *Avatar* fame; television icons Ed Asner, Tim Conway, Henry Winkler and Marlo Thomas; and C. Thomas Howell, who starred in the 1980s teen coming-of-age film *The Outsiders*. Other interviews feature Mike Love and Brian Wilson of the Beach Boys, Hank Williams Jr., Melissa Etheridge, George Jones, Rick Springfield, Sheryl Underwood, author Anne Rice, famed photographer Carol M. Highsmith, former New York City mayor Ed Koch, high-profile forensic pathologist/consultant Dr. Cyril Wecht and many others.

The *Montgomery Advertiser* and *Shelby Living Magazine* have written articles highlighting Marc and Melissa's success as founders of *Smashing Interviews Magazine*. The couple just recently celebrated their eighteenth wedding anniversary, and they currently reside in Birmingham, Alabama.